D0752756

Where's The Faith

WHAT WALKING IN FAITH REALLY LOOKS LIKE. SPOILER ALERT – SOMETIMES IT REALLY, REALLY SUCKS

BY

JODIE AUSTIN

Copyright © 2018 by Jodie Austin

All rights reserved. No part of this publication may be reproduced, distributed, or transmitted in any form or by any means, including photocopying, recording, or other electronic or mechanical methods, without the prior written permission of the publisher, except in the case of brief quotations embodied in critical reviews and certain other noncommercial uses permitted by copyright law. For permission requests, email the publisher at office@epiclifeministries.net. Please include "Attention: Permission Requests" in the subject line.

Printed in the United States of America 2018

Table of Contents

INTRODUCTION

Faith is hard. Faith is tough. I struggle with faith. Faith is an EVERDAY battle for me. I strive to live a life of faith, but I fail…OFTEN! I am NOT an expert on faith.

Okay, full-disclosure: 20 years ago, when God called me into the ministry and a life of teaching, it was with the complete understanding that I would always be very real, very raw, and very open. He used the words "full transparency." That is how I teach, that is how I live, and that is how I write. It's not always fun or easy, but it sure keeps people from putting me on some unattainable pedestal. My goal is to always keep people from focusing on fallible me (because I will always disappoint) but instead to keep them focusing ONLY on the infallible Father.

Soooooo… I will be fully upfront, open, and honest with you. God has called me to write this book. He's been calling me to write a book for years now. However, I had ZERO desire to write one, so I didn't. When I didn't listen to His instructions, He sent person after person after prophetic person to tell me that God said, write a book. "BUT I DON'T WANNA!", I would scream in a child-like temper tantrum. Maybe I didn't scream out loud, but I definitely screamed it internally. Still, the prophetic words kept coming. They came so often and from the most random sources that it almost became comical. But I still didn't want to write a book... so I didn't.

In all fairness, there were multiple reasons why I didn't want to write one. We won't go into ALL of those reasons because that would take a book all on its own. However, I will give you two of my excuses I used. I chose these two excuses to share because one is the pettiest excuse I often used, while the other is the most valid excuse I used.

Petty Excuse - I LITERALLY only use two fingers on each hand to type. My husband says I look like a crab hacking away at a keyboard. It will take me FOREVER to type a book! (Side note: They offered typing in high school as an elective. I chose not to take it because I assumed my secretary would type everything for me. My secretary? Ha! The high hopes and cockiness of a teenager! If you are wondering how all that worked out for me, I just typed that whole paragraph with only four out of ten fingers.) In my best moments, I essentially tried to pass this excuse off as a time management issue.

Valid Excuse: This is actually the excuse that prevented me from putting pen to paper for so long (or rather four fingers to keyboard). The excuse? I'm no expert! You must be an expert at something in order to write, right? Yes, I've been in the ministry for twenty years, but I am an expert at nothing. As a matter of fact, whenever I preach, I can often be heard talking about what a hot, mess I am or how I'm preaching to myself just as much as I'm preaching to the congregation. But in most of the Christian books I've read, the authors have it all figured out, meaning they are experts. They tell you exactly how to get to where you want to be in your walk with the Lord by simply following these expert tips written by the expert author and worded in an expert way. And I'm no expert. And yet, the prophetic words kept coming.

As I continued to stubbornly contest writing a book by giving God my valid and invalid excuses, He continued to ignore my protests by telling me what He wanted the book that I didn't want to write to be about. And man was it a doozy. He told me in the clearest verbiage possible that it was to be about…FAITH! Faith? Faith?!!!? Really? Are you kidding me? If I am close to being an expert at anything, it is NOT faith.

I gave God all my excuses. He didn't care. He said write a book. And I knew, as I had from the moment that He first said write one, that my preferences and my excuses meant nothing when He was requiring something of me. I couldn't stand being in disobedience. My heart is to please Him even if my will is stubborn. My heart is to be obedient to Him even if nothing in me wants to. My heart is to simply love Him and His people. So, here I am, writing this book out of pure love and obedience… about faith. And while I am no expert on faith, God is.

CHAPTER 1

YOU WANT ME TO DO WHAT?

I felt it creeping up on me again. I felt it consuming me...all of me. I recognized this thing. I wore it for so long that I thought it was just a part of my personality. I operated with it just like I operate my lungs, automatically. It was just a piece of me. It was who I was-- who I had been for years. I had been angry and bitter for so long that I didn't even know who I would be without it. Bitterness...yes, and I wore it well.

Let me start from the beginning. I have to believe that God has an extreme sense of humor. While He had been telling me to write a book for years, He only voiced the topic of the book a few months ago. Now, that may not seem like a big deal UNTIL you look at the season in which it was communicated. The timing of it could not have been worse!! We were in one of the lowest, darkest times of our lives and God comes out and says I want you to write a book about faith. What?!!!? Really? While my own faith is being tested beyond belief and is at its bottom, You are telling me to write a book about faith? While I am questioning if You are even hearing me as I cry out to You, You are telling me to write a book about faith? While I am on the verge of mental and spiritual collapse, You are telling me to write a book about faith? And He simply replied…Yes.

Maybe a little background to paint the picture of where we were at the time will help you understand. Until recently, my husband and I had been working at a local church as Associate Pastors. We were there for a little over two years. Man, oh man, what a ride it was! This church had absolutely been through the wringer. When we had been there for only about three months, a fellow staff pastor was abruptly fired for inappropriate sexual contact with a minor. We were brand new to the church and still trying to get our legs underneath us. Clearly, this news was quite a shock.

Still, God told us to stay. We had been there for only about six months when the church lost its Senior Pastor of **eighteen** years suddenly and without warning, due to moral failure-- eighteen years of the same man at the helm and eighteen years' worth of trust and leadership gone overnight. Many left. Still, God told us to stay.

One month later, still reeling from the previous loss, the last remaining Staff Pastor (other than us) began to spread viscous lies about us, malicious, brutal, unsubstantiated lies. At this point, most of the people knew us and our character so all lies were quickly proven to be false, and he was promptly fired. We were now the last ones standing. Still, the sting of his words was pretty agonizing. What had we ever done that could possibly make someone say such nasty, hateful things about us? And still, God told us to stay.

Even though we had been in the ministry for 18 years at that point, we were new to this denomination. Because the District Superintendent did not know us very well at that point, he decided not to hand the church over to us. Yes, he made this decision-- even though we had successfully been senior pastors in the past, even though we had been tried and tested in the ministry, even though we had a proven ministerial track record, even though we had proven ourselves faithful through all the negativity and chaos, and even though we were the last ones standing.   But still, God told us to stay.

They ended up bringing in an interim pastor, in general, someone who comes in when a church is in turmoil. He stays for a year, gets it healthy and then turns it over to the new pastors. We stayed on as associate pastors. The church was so badly broken. As you can imagine, the congregation was a fraction of what it had started with. The remaining people were hurt, confused, and angry by all the changes and rightly so. We knew we needed to help bring healing for those people. We knew we had to rebuild. We knew we had to start fresh. We knew it was going to be a lot of work. We also knew we were the only staff.

The people were so wounded and damaged by the past events that getting people to volunteer for anything at the church was next to impossible. Who could blame them? What were they sowing their time into? No one knew if the church would even stay open. They didn't' know who was to fall next. There was zero trust as all trust had been broken by leaders in whom the congregation had placed all their trust previously. We understood that. So, we set out to bring healing and to gain trust.

Thankfully, we had one other couple that stepped up to serve and volunteer. They worked side-by-side and shoulder-to-shoulder with us. When it was all said and done, there wasn't a single aspect of the church that we weren't involved in. We wanted to rebuild for them. They deserved that. We were involved in worship team, tech, web design, graphics, conferences, youth ministry, women's ministry, children's ministry, interior design, teaching, counseling, serving on committees and our everyday pastoral duties. There was nothing going on at that church that we did not have our hands in. I say that with zero arrogance. This is not a place where I am trying insert bragging rights. This is simply meant to show all the areas that had once flourished with volunteers now lay in ruins and no one had the strength or the stamina to help rebuild. They couldn't; they needed to focus on healing themselves before they could focus on rebuilding the church.

We understood that. So, we jumped into action. We were beyond exhausted but knew this was where God had called us. I mean if He hadn't released us after all the turmoil we had been through in our short time there, we knew we were there for a divine purpose. And if that divine purpose was to help build a devastated church, then rebuild is what we would do. And to be honest, we counted it all as joy. This was a hurting church that needed our help, and that's what we were called to do. So, we dug deep, jumped in with both feet and began trying to raise up leaders to help us in the task.

With patience, compassion, and God's direction, we moved in the ministry according to what we believed the Lord told us to do, and with time, people began to heal. They began to trust. They truly saw us as their pastors, and we saw them as our people. For the next year, leadership and board members told us that the church would not survive if we were not appointed Senior Pastors.

The congregation had already dealt with so much loss that leaders felt they couldn't deal with losing us too. Everything functioned from that decision from that point on. This church would be handed over to us at the end of the interim pastor's one-year stint. The Interim Pastor even had us start making most of the decisions so that the church would start functioning as ours before he left. Everything was moving in the exact direction that we felt God was dictating.

The only downside was that we were only getting paid a part-time salary--no, not a part-time salary EACH but a part-time salary between the two of us. Still, that was okay because God had told us that this is where we were supposed to be.

We knew that even though we struggled, we were pouring into something that was in our future. We looked at it as an investment. So, we sold plasma. We sold our belongings. We did odd jobs. We went without. We borrowed money. We did whatever we needed to do to scrape by in order to help the church, the people, and the investment into our future.

In the meantime, the denomination's corporate headquarters handpicked 100 people nationwide that they saw as leaders that they really wanted to recognize and pour into. These were leaders that they thought would plant churches that would affect every zip code in the nation, 100 out of thousands. You guessed it; my husband and I were two of the 100. We were so honored. This was just a confirmation that we were in the right place, at the right time, and rightfully following God's direction.

We were told to write down our visions for church planting (when, where, how) and send it to headquarters so that they could pray over it daily. We were elated. Spreading God's word! Making disciples! That's who we are in a nutshell! We were so excited for the future. We had been through so much mayhem and confusion at this church that I often wondered why God did not release us from there. But now, it all makes sense. It was for such a time as this!!

Everything was going great, right? All according to plan? We thought so too. My husband and I were worked to the bone, literally working 60 to 80 hours a week. We only went home to sleep. The couple that used to laugh and talk endlessly about nothing now only talked about church related issues. Church had consumed so much of our lives that we really didn't have anything else to talk about. Our entire existence was church.

So, we were told by the Interim Pastor that we needed to take a vacation before he left, and we took over the church.

And we did! We ended up taking a two-week vacation. It was the first time in 20 years of ministry that we had been on vacation and missed TWO Sundays in a row. We felt a little naughty, a little guilty and whole lot of excitement!

As desperately as we needed the money, we needed to live and breathe and relax even more. We ended up using an income tax return to fund our vacation. You would be surprised the fun adventure you can have on a budget (Groupon is my best friend).

Looking forward to our first two-week vacation ever, we loaded up and headed out. We ended up spending one week with family and one week of adventure by ourselves. After our relaxing, rejuvenating, no responsibilities week with our family, we headed off to the adventure part of our vacation. It was going to be a week of amusement parks, thrill rides, and adrenaline rushes.

So, we leave our family and head out to San Antonio, Texas. It was supposed to be our very first day of fun and thrills. We woke up at the hotel excited for our day. Miraculously, I beat my husband getting dressed. Innocently enough, I decided to check my email, something I typically do every single morning. But that day was going to be anything but typical. As I sat there on the end of the bed at a hotel in San Antonio, Texas, my entire life was changed in an instant—by email.

Speechless, I just sat there motionless. I lost all color. My husband knew something was wrong just by looking at me. He grabbed my phone to see what had happened. Right there in black and white, everything that we were promised, everything we had hoped for and everything that we had worked tirelessly for was taken in an instant…BY EMAIL.

The email read, "The board has decided to keep the interim pastor for another year. I know this is not what has been talked about or discussed previously but the decision is final. It is certainly our desire to pay you more, but until we get completely up to date on our mortgage payments, I don't anticipate significant additional financial support."

We were devastated. What about the promises made to us? What happened? We've only been gone a week. How could so much change in a week? Everything was fine when we left. We were making most of the decisions for the church, and, for the most part, the board and the congregation were happy with the direction that the church was going. Did we do something wrong? Were we being accused of something? Our minds were spinning out of control. Something BIG had to have happened for such a drastic change in the decision-making process, right? But what was it? Was it us? We didn't know, and we couldn't ask because we were given this overwhelming news...by email...on the first day of our vacation.

Just the day before, my husband and I talked about how excited we were that our financial struggles were almost over. The interim pastor would leave, and we would get his salary (which was substantially more than ours). We talked about what we would do with it, how we would spend it and how we could pour it back into the church. We were just excited at the thought of paying our bills ON TIME, buying groceries, and maybe even a date night here and there. But clearly, as stated in the email, that was not going to happen-- the anticipation of living a life without lack and struggle and plasma donations …taken in an instant…by email.

We thought about everything we had poured into that church, into those people-- a years' worth of 60 to 80-hour work weeks for part-time pay and we weren't even worth a phone call. Two years' worth of faithfulness through the craziest of circumstances and we weren't worth a phone call? We found out by email…on the first day of our vacation, by email. How were we worth so little?

All we wanted to do was process this information, curl up on a couch, and cry and pray. Unfortunately, everything on the vacation had already been paid for so we had to follow through with the plans. I honestly didn't even know that you could feel so heartbroken, betrayed, saddened, and confused in the middle of an amusement park surrounded by screaming, happy people. There are no words to describe that feeling.

When we got back from our vacation, things got ugly. We were gone for only two weeks. What in the world happened during our absence? Accusations and lies were rampant. The Board made decisions without consulting the congregation. Heck, the board made decisions without ever even consulting us, not once. We were never even asked if the accusations being brought against us were true. As a matter of fact, the board never once brought us in and asked us anything. That's still crazy to me. Hadn't we at least proven ourselves worthy of questioning?

To make a long story short, within three months of returning from vacation, we were let go. Let go? It's still so strange to write those words. We've never been let go from anywhere in our entire lives. Even more confusing, we were just so certain that this place was supposed to be in our future, not our past. But now, we were let go. How in the world did this happen? Still to this day, I'm not exactly sure why. You get a different answer depending on who you ask. Some say the interim pastor turned the board against us; some say the DS bad mouthed us; some say the DS did nothing but defend us;

some defended our character; and others slaughtered it. It was just a horrible, heartbreaking situation that I never saw coming.

I was left so confused. What had we ever done that would have led to this place. Moral failure? Lack of leadership? Insubordination? Teaching bad theology? We hadn't done any of those things so why? We had seen so many people rightfully terminated from their positions at this church for the corrupt, sinful, immoral things they had done to others. How were we now in the same position as they were? We had done nothing wrong. I can honestly say that we served that church with integrity, faith, obedience, and a love for the Father and His people. We certainly weren't perfect, but we strived for excellence with every fiber of our beings. So how could it have gone so wrong? The hardest part is that we still don't really have any answers.

If I'm being honest, it STILL hurts a little. I poured every piece of myself into that place, into those people. We loved those people so much. We still do. I know without a shadow of a doubt that God called us to that church. I know that when all hell broke loose time and time again that God told us to stay at that church. I know that everything that we sowed into that church was at God's directive.

I was pretty confused by God at this point. Everything that we did at the church and for the church was done in faith. And yet this was our repayment? Why? We lived and moved and breathed faith through this whole process. We stayed when we wanted to run at YOUR directive, God. We stayed when we couldn't pay our bills at Your directive, God. We worked ourselves into exhaustion at Your directive, God. And for what? Is this where faith gets us? Is this the reward for being faithful to you and your people? We are left with nothing because of our faith!!! And now You want me to write about it?

CHAPTER 2

DON'T PITCH YOUR TENT IN HELL

The level at which I hurt scared me. It was the kind of hurt that changes a person. It was the kind of hurt that turns into bitterness. And if I wasn't already bitter, I surely was close.

We didn't have a lot of time to process what had happened as our only source of income was about to stop. It may not have been much, but it was something. Now that "something" was about to disappear.

I was probably more emotional in that next month than I had been in my entire life. I was so angry and hurt and confused. I felt equally betrayed by God and the people of the church. After all, I had trusted them all completely.

The truth is, even though I was angry and frustrated at God, I did not want to separate myself from Him. I've been there and done that. I've been bitter before. Young adult me was a miserable human being living a miserable life and causing misery to those around me.

Even though I was only angry and bitter at one specific person, looking back, I realize that my anger and bitterness grew like a cancer and affected everyone that I loved because I became so cold and callous.

It caused me to harden my heart to everyone, including God, even though that was never my intention.

I thought it was something I could control. We all do. We all think that we can harbor anger or unforgiveness for just one person without it affecting us, our relationships, or even our walk with God. We think we can just fence off that area of our heart, brain, and spirit from the rest of us. But we aren't wired like that.

That's why we have women that hate men. They were hurt by a man and became angry and bitter. But instead of just hating 'that' man, they start to hate all men. That root of bitterness was allowed to stay, and so it grew at a wildfire's pace. No little girl has ever aspired to grow up and become a man-hater (Or vice versa for men). She was not born that way. So, what happened? Bitterness happened. She thought she could contain it, but again, that's not how our bodies are wired.

That's why we have so many addicts. Yes, addiction can be hereditary, but science is now showing that the addiction gene is triggered by trauma: trauma that isn't dealt with or coped with; trauma that causes anger, hurt, and bitterness that consumes them; and trauma that changes their coping mechanism. That trauma harbored an unforgiving heart and spirit, and it grew out of control. But no child has ever aspired to grow up and become an addict. So, what happened? Bitterness happened.

That's one of the reasons why we have so many people who are angry for no reason. We run into them every day, at the office, in traffic, at the bank, and in the grocery store. You haven't personally done anything to them, but they are rude, mean, and vile to everyone around them, including you. Why? They are angry. They are angry at the world. Someone hurt them at some point in their lives, and they harbored that unforgiving bitterness. Now it has affected them to their core. Everyone is affected by it. But no one has ever aspired to grow up and be a miserable human being that spews misery on others. So, what happened? Bitterness happened.

Marriages are affected by bitterness, churches are split because of bitterness, friendships are lost because of bitterness, and lives are taken too soon because of bitterness. I could go on and on.

Hebrews 12:15 says, *See to it that no one falls short of the grace of God and that no bitter root grows up to cause trouble and defile many.*

Even scripture tells us that many will be defiled just by the root of bitterness. So, I encourage you, no, I beg of you, that if there is any unforgiveness in you at all, please deal with it by any means necessary. Whether it be through counseling, prayer or just through introspective work—DO IT and do it NOW. Not because they deserve forgiveness, but because you and your loved ones deserve to be free from the effects of it.

I have been there and done that. As I said before, I recognized bitterness. I even took pride in it. I wore my bitterness like some kind of badge of honor. I was tough as nails and needed no one. But I was miserable. And I soon realized that my 'needing no one attitude" had come to include God. And that was never my intention. It took a lot of counseling, prayer and seeking God's face, but I was able to receive healing and be delivered from that. I don't want to go back. I can never go back. But it was happening, as if I were being embraced in it. Since my deliverance, I knew freedom and joy. But now, the hurt was so unbearable that it seemed unescapable. And for that reason alone, I knew it had to be dealt with. I did not want to live in an inescapable prison of bitterness ever again. It's a prison that can be extremely difficult to escape. A prison that I had already fought my way out of. A prison that I had already been delivered from. I don't ever want to go back to that prison. So, I dealt with my anger and frustration at both God and man.

Saying that I dealt with my anger and frustration makes it sound so easy and simple. It was actually anything but. It was not quick or instantaneous. It was not easy; it was hard. It was not simple; it was excruciatingly difficult. It was a process, a painful process, something I had to walk out.

It was something I had to make a conscious decision to do every single day; I had to decide –make a decision—whether I wanted to or not or whether I felt like it or not. It was a decision to simply keep trudging onward.

I knew I had to keep moving forward while I was in the process of healing. I also knew that stagnation is dangerous. And as angry as I was, I knew it would be a bad, bad time for me to choose to be stagnant, to just wallow in my feelings.

I was so hurt that my pain was even in my prayers. "God, please help me to want to want to forgive them," because even though I knew I needed to, I didn't want to.

Somehow and quite slowly, I began to feel healing. I began to quote Romans 8:31:

If God is for us then who can be against us.

I had to remind myself that even if the whole world was against me, my God was for me. But to be honest, because I felt a little betrayed by God during all of this, I needed this scripture to remind me that God was still for me. I quoted it often to get it in my spirit, and I once again began seeking comfort and guidance from the Father. I realized that God had not abandoned us. I realized that God did not take us through this for no reason. I realized that there are times in life where things will be unrightfully stolen from us because people have their own free will. But most importantly, I realized that no matter what is stolen from us, God is a God of restoration---that what was taken from us will be given back seven-fold.

So even though the rug of my life had been pulled out from underneath me, I was ready to get back into my spiritual saddle. No, I still didn't have any answers, but I knew I did not want to stay here.

Something my grandma used to say stuck in my head and would play almost continuously on a loop: *If you're going through hell, don't stop and pitch a tent there; you just keep right on moving."*

What I had just walked through surely felt a little like hell. But all I knew was I wanted that hell to be over. I knew I could not allow my hurt and anger to cause me to set up camp there. I needed it to be in my past and not in my present or my future, and the only way to ensure that happened was to let it go. So, I fought. I fought hard. I fought like I was the third monkey trying to get on Noah's Ark. It was a deliberate fight. Daily I had to take captive those thoughts that sprang up inside me, trying to ignite that bitterness again. God instructed me to begin to declare blessings over each and every single individual that had hurt or betrayed me at the church. Then He instructed me to repeat these blessings every single day until I actually meant them. I began to praise and thank God that He had better things in store for me. Again, I had to repeat it until I believed it. I began to remind myself of all the prophetic words that had been spoken over me.

Why was I doing these things? Because I had been so damaged by the church events that all of God's promises felt so far out of my reach, I had to speak the words that God instructed me to because I needed to build my spirit back up. Even if my own ears didn't believe the words that were coming out of my mouth, my spirit did! I needed to straighten my spiritual backbone. I needed to re-engage my faith. I wanted to move forward. I needed to move forward. I did my absolute best to move forward.

But then I found that despite my best efforts, there were still days that my best just wasn't enough. Finally, it dawned on me that that was okay, too.

CHAPTER 3

TASTE THOSE WORDS BEFORE SPITTING THEM OUT

So…here we are. It has been four months since the church let us go—the same church that was promised to us. We are no closer today to understanding why than we were the day that it happened. We've had four months to deal with the hurt, betrayal, and confusion. And truth be told, I am so much better, but still not 100% completely healed. I'm not afraid to admit that. I have my good days and my better days. But it still hurts.

If God had vindicated me within those four months, I would probably be completely healed. If God had radically changed our finances in those four months proving to us and others that we ARE blessed, I would probably be completely healed. If God had completely silenced my enemies in those four months, I would probably be completely healed. Yeah, four months might have been long enough to completely heal IF God had acted in a time and fashion that I found appropriate. If only He would do as I see fit. It sounds ridiculous when you read it like that, doesn't it? Yet we put those boundaries on God every day when His timing turns out to be different from ours.

When life's proverbial rug gets pulled out from under us, we almost always run to the Father for His comfort and guidance. Our hearts may not be completely healed, and we still may be processing through the trauma, but we still run to the Father.

That part is good. **THAT** is what we are supposed to do. The problem is we end up putting our HUMAN expectations into the midst of it. And that, my friends, is where things start to go horribly wrong for us.

What do I mean by that? I mean we think we have it all figured out. We KNOW what God is going to do and how He is going to do it. God is going to vindicate me IMMEDIATELY.

God is going to get my job back ASAP. God is going to make them pay for what they've done INSTANTLY. God is going to right all the wrongs done to me PROMPTLY.

But here's the truth. We always start off strong. The hurt, or confusion, or devastation drives us into the arms of the Father (as it should). We start off on fire! Faith beams out of us like rays of sunshine. We are righteously angry, and we are fighting for what's ours.

The problem comes when things don't happen when we think they should. God works within the confines of eternity, not time. Time is a man-made element. Our 24-hour, clock-driven existence means nothing to Him. So as the hours turn into days, days into weeks, weeks into months and sometimes months into years, our faith starts to wane. And far too often, as our faith starts to diminish, our flesh begins to rise. We are angry, bitter, and confused. We are angry at the world, and, if we are truly honest with ourselves, we are angry at God. We have gone from shooting fiery rays of faith to shooting off nothing but our mouths. And what's coming out of our mouths is anything but faith.

Yup, God didn't move when we thought He should or how we thought He should, and now we are ten different kinds of angry.

Hebrews 11:1 says, *Now faith is the substance of things hoped for, the evidence of things not seen.*

We all know that scripture. We've all recited that scripture. But depending on what we are walking through and how long we have been walking, our feelings can drastically differ. There are times when that scripture stirs up our faith and causes us to dig in and stand a little taller and straighter while we are believing for the things not yet seen.

But then again, if we are to be real honest with ourselves, there are times in our lives when that scripture stirs up more frustration than it does faith. "Faith? Hope? Ha! Laughable! There is no hope! God, I had faith and hope and, yet I am STILL at the bottom of the well!!! What good does faith or hope do us if we are still drowning?" How many of you reading this book have ever felt that way or feel this way right now?

When we sink into that hopeless place of despair, we have now entered what is known as *hope deferred*. And man, if I had to name one of the enemy's most efficient weapons used against us, hope deferred would be at the top of the list. When you are dealing with hope deferred, you have lost all fight in you. You see the fight as being useless anyway. Hope deferred says that all the promises that you've been given by God and all the prophetic words you've received by God's people, will never be seen. They will always be just out of reach. It says that nothing ever works out anyway so why keep trying.

And THAT is exactly why it is such a valuable tool of the enemy. He doesn't even have to worry about us if we have taken ourselves out of the fight. He basically just sets us aside on a shelf somewhere and lets us self-destruct. Hope deferred makes his job a whole lot easier.

Over the years, I have heard so many people refer to Satan as dumb, foolish, or simple. And that is quite unfortunate. You should never underestimate your enemy. He is smart. He is deviously smart. He has been at this game for years.

He knows what works, and like any good and wise enemy, he knows to strike when you're exhausted, when you're weak, when he sees a kink in the armor. And I hate to say it, but it is an excellent and effective strategy. He will almost always attack the hardest when we are at our lowest and weakest. A weak target is an easy target. I said he was smart, not honorable.

Proverbs 13:12 says, *Hope deferred makes the heart sick, but a longing fulfilled is a tree of life.*

Hope deferred literally makes your heart sick according to this scripture. I need you to really let that sink in for a second. **HOPE DEFERRED MAKES THE HEART SICK**. Those are powerful words. Those are compelling words. Those are TERRIFYING words!

Yet so many of us walk in hope deferred for far too long, years even. But some don't get the gravity of these words. Some believe they DESERVE to feel this way.

For these people, the situation feels hopeless and inescapable. Plus, they feel that they did everything they were supposed to do. They feel as if God is the one that's not holding up His end of the bargain, right?

And if we get super real, raw, and honest, it FEELS good to be mad. We don't want to do what is right because then that may require us to not be angry anymore…and we WANT to be angry. We DESERVE to be angry. We will be un-angry when God delivers us! Am I right? The problem is this little scripture of Luke 6:45:

"A good man brings good things out of the good stored up in his heart, and an evil man brings evil things out of the evil stored up in his heart. For the mouth speaks what the heart is full of."

Ouch!! What is your heart full of? Proverbs 18:21 says:

The tongue has the power of life and death, and those who love it will eat its fruit.

Now, let's look at those scriptures together. *For the mouth speaks what the heart is full of and the tongue has the power of life and death.*

So, if our tongue, which holds the power of life or death, speaks what is in your heart, and your heart just so happens to be full of frustration, despair, and hopelessness, what are you speaking over your life, over your children, over your marriage, over your situation?

If you look at the second part of Proverbs 18:21, it says, *"and those who love it will eats its fruit."* What does that mean? Let's put it in our modern-day lingo. This scripture is very simply saying there are consequences to your words.

Our words are powerful. When God created the heavens and the earth, how did He do it? Did He scream or yell or jump through hoops? No. He SPOKE them into existence using only His words. And because He lives in us and through us, our words CREATE; they have

39

power. You are either speaking blessings or curses over your own life depending on what is coming out of your own mouth.

Are we creating galaxies or planets? Of course not! We do not have the authority to do that. But you do CREATE within your realm of authority. And you create simply by speaking.

They have done scientific studies on controlled plant groups that were grown under the exact same conditions. There was only one difference between the two controlled groups. One group received positivity and praise. The other group received curses and negativity. And even though both groups were given the exact same amount of food, water and sunlight, only the group with positive affirmations spoken over them flourished.

Look at what our words do to our children. Our children are within our realm of authority. We can either break them with our words or mend them with our words.

Guarding what is in your heart and coming out of your mouth is so important that the Bible is chocked full of scripture after scripture containing warning after warning regarding this very thing.

Matthew 12:37: For by your words you will be acquitted, and by your words you will be condemned."
Proverbs 10:19: When there are many words, transgression is unavoidable, but he who restrains his lips is wise.

Proverbs 12:13: An evil man is ensnared by the transgression of his lips, but the righteous will escape from trouble.
Proverbs 13:3: The one who guards his mouth preserves his life; the one who opens wide his lips comes to ruin.

Proverbs 21:23: He who guards his mouth and his tongue, Guards his soul from troubles.

What are all these scriptures saying? They are saying that in all things, choose your words wisely. Words have such a powerful effect. Your words are powerful. Your words create.

Your words condemn. Your words kill but they can heal as well. Your words tear down, and your words build.

We create within our realms of authority. And the scripture I referred to earlier says, **"that the mouth speaks what the heart is full of."** So, ask yourself, what exactly are you creating? What exactly is your heart full of?

It doesn't feel so good to be angry now, does it? Knowing that it can affect your children, your spouse, your job, your church and every other area that falls under your realm of authority changes things a little bit, doesn't it? But here's the thing; you are going to get angry. You are going to be angry at people, and you might even get angry at God.

For some reason, we have been taught in the church that if you are angry, you are sinning. But God gave us our emotions. Each emotion is created for a specific purpose. Sometimes that purpose is simply to let you know that you are off track. So, it's okay to be angry. It's okay to be human. It's okay to fail sometimes. But it's not okay to stay there. The sin is to stay there.

Hope deferred is the killer of faith. But faith is necessary to live the life that we are called to live. So, hope deferred must die even though that is no easy task.

CHAPTER 4

OUCH! THAT BLESSING REALLY HURT

Somewhere in our walk, we have all wanted the Red Sea experience, that instantaneous deliverance from our enemies. But please, for the love of all that's holy, please be careful what you ask for because that's EXACTLY what we got-- the Israelite experience.

Here is the thing about me. I whole-heartedly recognize just how hard it is to kill "hope deferred." I do not speak those words lightly. And I never speak on anything out of theory; it's always out of experience. I, unfortunately, have had more than my fair share of hope deferred in my lifetime. I even find it ironic that God is requiring me to write about faith while I am battling my hardest to stave off doubt even as we speak.

The past four months since we were let go from the church had been beyond trying. Those words don't even seem to do it justice. What we have been through has been absolutely wearisome. We erroneously thought that when the whole church fiasco was over that the worst was behind us. Unfortunately, that wasn't so.

Getting back to the Red Sea, let me explain what I mean by that. When we were let go from the church, we had absolutely no idea what we were going to do for finances. Miraculously, we got the break of a lifetime…kind of. We kind of got the Red Sea experience. Hurricane Irma had just hit Florida. While the hurricane itself was horrible, it opened up a new opportunity for us, an amazing opportunity that paid tremendously well. We were told that they would be looking for Independent Claims Adjusters from all over the nation because the damage was far too great for the Florida workers to handle. Claims

Adjusters make bank! Yes, this was our break. THIS was why we were let go from the church, right—So, God could bless us financially? Now it all made sense! We were so excited!

We knew someone who had been in the business for 17 years and he thought he would be able to get us work. We waited to hear when we should start our trip for Florida. Then we waited some more. We waited some more, and we waited some more. Even our friend with 17 years of experience was having a hard time finding work because so many adjusters jumped on the opportunity.

Thankfully, another adjustment company picked us up. They said they would have more than enough work for us. We were thrilled. We began packing and preparing to leave. But the next day, the job opportunity fell through with no explanation. We were upset but not deterred. We simply prayed.

The very next day, we ran into a longtime family friend who was in the business and had been for years. He said he would snatch us up right away. They had more than enough work for us. We thought THAT's why the other job fell through. We were supposed to work for our friend that we knew and trusted! We were beyond excited.

He stated that he could give us thirty claims right off the bat, and that was just to get us started. We simply just needed to call him the next day to set everything up. That was around 7:00pm on a Thursday night. By Friday morning, the news was different. In less than 24 hours, everything had changed. He told us that, so many people had jumped on the bandwagon that all the job opportunities were drying up almost overnight. He was deeply sorry…so were we.

We are from Colorado, but we were in Texas at the time with family. While there, I asked for wisdom and discernment. Do we go back to Colorado or will we be sent to Florida? As I was sitting on the bed at my in-law's house, I heard God tell us to start driving to Florida. Wait, what? Come again! Someone with 17 years' worth of experience can't find work! How on the earth are two newbies going to pull this off?

But after talking to my husband and hearing that God had told him the same thing, we prepared to head out. (Funny side note: God told my husband before He told me. My husband was hesitant to tell me because well, it sounded crazy. Long story short, God HAD to tell me because my husband wouldn't!)

So, we took our last check that we got from the church and we headed to Florida. We were so afraid. That last check was all the money we had in the world. And that was supposed to be used to pay our rent. But God said go...and so we did.

We drove all the way to Tallahassee, Florida, where we stayed for two days. We were making phone calls, trying to establish connections, and also staying in touch with our friend who was still trying to find us work. Nothing! Absolutely nothing! But God, you told us BOTH that we were to go.

The next morning, my husband looked at me. Feeling tired and defeated, he said, "Let's go home." I have to tell you, those words terrified me. My husband has more faith than anyone I know. In the bleakest and darkest of times, he is a steadfast rock of faith. So, to see that rock crack ever so slightly, I began to panic inside. Oh no! What have we done? Now we have no money for rent and just enough money to make it back to Colorado. We will return to nothing and with nothing.

But there was the tiniest bit of faith that broke through my fear. I don't even know if it was quite the size of a mustard seed. I reminded my husband that God told us BOTH, independently of each other, to go to Florida. He did not bring us here to abandon us. The next words out of my husband's mouth will stick with me forever. He said, "OK. Let's go. If we fail, we will fail big. We will fail by trying and not by forfeit."

The very next day, we got the call from our friend. He had found us work! YES!!! Our faith had pulled us through! We celebrated with pats on the back about what good Christians we were, good, faithful Christians who never gave up. And because we never gave up, we will now be rewarded! Spiritual high-fives all around!

So, we left Tallahassee and headed to Sarasota where our work would be. We got there, checked into our hotel, and thanked God for His provision before we went to sleep. We woke up the next morning only to be told once again that the job had fallen through. We were told that they were supposed to get more work, but the work dried up almost overnight. So much for those spiritual high-fives!

I was speechless. My faith was built up over and over again just to be shredded and thrown to the ground. Wow. Why, God? What are you doing to me? What is going on? I have had faith. I have been obedient. What more can I do? I was at such a loss for words that night that I just had to let my tears speak for me.

We ended up staying in Sarasota, Florida, for about five days, still making phone calls, still trying to make connections, and still trying to have faith and stand on the word that God gave us. We couldn't deny the fact that He had told us both to come. So, we stood on that, shakily, but we stood.

Finally, on day five, our friend called. He was on his way to Florida, and he had found a company that had over 70 claims waiting for each of us. That may not seem like a lot, but those 70 claims would provide more for us financially than many get paid in a year.

The job was in Ft. Lauderdale. So, we packed up once again and headed even farther from home. Each leg of this trip and each failed job had taken us farther and farther from home all while costing us money that we did not have.

But there we were, trying to be faithful and heading to Ft. Lauderdale. I will tell you that that was the hardest leg of the trip, each mile that we went, fighting the fear that this job too would be pulled the second we pulled up. All we could say was, "If we fail, we will fail big. We will fail being obedient."

We got to Fort Lauderdale and the job was waiting on us!!! All 70 claims! That is more than any other company had ever offered us. Was that why all the other jobs fell through?

Had God wanted to bless us financially with 70 instead of 30? God, thank you! Finally! Our faith had paid off!! We now knew why He brought us!! All of the heartache was at least worth it now!

When I relay that event to you, doesn't it give you the warm fuzzies all over? We were rewarded for our faith. THOSE are the stories we like to hear, right—the ones where everything worked out almost exactly according to plan? Oh man, if only that's how the story ended.

We immediately got our claims and started to work. Unfortunately, the guy who was over us was probably one of the meanest, evil, vile people I have ever had the displeasure of working for, just brutally degrading. If we asked a question because we didn't know the answer, we were told how dumb we were. If we tried to figure it out so we didn't have to ask for help and made a mistake, we were told how dumb you were. Every day was filled with new threats and intimidation. We were constantly being threatened to have our files pulled from us and given to someone else, even though we had already done the work.

The stress was unbelievable. We were leaving the rented condo at 7:00 am returning, at about 8:00 pm and working on paperwork until about 3:00 am. I wish I could say that we walked through the stress perfectly, but I can't. My blood pressure was through the roof. My muscles in my neck and back were in painful knots. And to top it all off, my husband and I were at each other's throats. But through it all, we were still just so thankful for the opportunity.

We made it through it. We survived the attacks and intimidation. We weathered the stress, and after a month in Florida, we were finally on our way home to beautiful Colorado. However, we still hadn't been paid, so we had to borrow money to make it back home. No worries though, we knew the windfall was coming!

Remember the money I was talking about earning from this job? We ended up making close to $50,000, such a tremendous blessing. $50,000 in one month! That made all the stress, intimidation and threats worth it!!

We got our first check on November 22, a little less than a month from when we left Florida. It was our 20th wedding anniversary as well. It was a great surprise!

The amount was substantial. It was about $25,000, half of what we were owed. We paid off a lot of debt. We repaid all the money that we had to borrow during our trip to Florida. We tithed. We paid three months' rent. We caught up on all of our bills. And we were able to get things in order financially.

We had planned to use the next check that we got, to live off and pay everyday bills while we put some things together business wise. The company that we worked for in Florida said that their paydays were on the 1st and 15th. That meant our next check should arrive on December 1st.

But it didn't. I thought, "No worries; it will be here on the 15th. Nope, no check. Hmmmm, January 1st? Nope. January 15th? Think again. It had been over two months since our last paycheck--three months since we turned in our last files yet, still no money.

Fast forward to today. Because we paid off so much debt, under the assumption that we were to be paid regularly, we are left with nothing. When I say we ended up with nothing, I mean absolutely nothing. Actually, we have less than nothing. Our bank accounts are overdrawn. We had to borrow money for food. We had to borrow money for our car payment. Unfortunately, we can't actually drive the car because the insurance has lapsed. And every single bill we have is past due. And to top it all off, our phones just got shut off.

My faith has landed me in a whole heap of misery. Like I said, if you are looking to read a book by someone that has it all figured out, then this isn't for you. But if you are looking to read a book by someone who has learned to find faith in the middle of life's chaos and crap, I just might be your girl. If you are looking to learn from someone who has had to dig herself out of a deep situational-depression and fight her way back to faith, this might be the book for you.

Just a quick side note. I am writing this book in real time and in the middle of the chaos.

I'm not writing this after coming out on the other side and already knowing the outcome. I am still beyond broke. I am still behind in bills. I'm still having to borrow money for food. My cell phone is still turned off. Yet, I still don't believe that any of that disqualifies me from writing this book. Faith is only faith if you have it in the midst of the storm. It's easy to have faith when you're in the palace. But true faith is proven in the pit. So, while this pit sucks beyond belief, my faith will stand.

CHAPTER 5

MR. LION, WHAT BIG TEETH YOU HAVE

It's a Friday morning, and I just rolled out of bed. I did what I do every morning: I stumble into the kitchen, make some coffee, and check my bank account balance on my phone. Every single weekday morning I wake up with so much hope that today is the day. I imagine looking at my bank account and seeing the $25,000 that is owed to us in our account: the $25,000 that is rightfully mine; the $25,000 that we worked so incredibly hard for; the $25,000 that we stepped out into faith to get; the $25,000 that we so desperately need. WE SO DESPERATELY NEED IT!

But, it's not there. I've spent the last sixty days doing the same routine, starting the day with such hope only to have that hope crushed before I've even finished my morning coffee. Every morning so far, I have been greeted with a -$143 balance. Fridays are the worst. I know with absolute certainty that if it's not there on Friday morning, I have to wait until Monday to have another chance at a deposit being made. I'm probably the only person on the planet that looks forward to Mondays.

The longer we went without money, the more dire our situation became. I had been sick for over a month, like really sick. I desperately needed to go to the doctor. Cold? Flu? Sinus infection? Pneumonia? I didn't know but it just would't go away. Still, I couldn't go to the doctor because I didn't have the money. Even if I went to the ER, I couldn't afford the prescriptions the doctors would prescribe. So, on top of being broke and having to depend on everyone else for our survival, I was absolutely miserable and a little concerned for my health at this point. This was EXACTLY what I needed right now, right?

Imagine this scenario: Every morning I must actively fight hope deferred. Some days I do better than others. Some days I just lie on the couch. Some days I think – if this is where faith gets me, I can do bad all by myself.

Yet, I won't allow myself to stay there for long. I know where I will end up if I stop believing, stop praying, and stop praising. I know where I will end up if I attempt to do this on my own. I've been there and done that. I ended up so depressed that I could barely function. I've actually been so hopeless and so depressed that I tried to take my own life. Then after I had kids, the only reason I took suicide off the table was because I didn't want my kids to be the ones to find my body. THAT is what happens to ME when I lose hope. THAT is what happens to ME when I lose faith. THAT is what happens to ME when I try to go it alone. And THAT is what happens to me when I allow myself to stay in hope deferred wallowing in my misery.

And it all started with being spiritually exhausted. Then the exhaustion ushered in a sliver of hopelessness. Then that hopelessness blossomed into hope deferred: the idea that nothing ever works out anyway so why even bother because things will never get better.

I'm only referencing the last two years of my life and the struggles I faced during those 24 months. If I went into my whole life…well, that would be a book in and of itself. So, with so much heartache, so much trauma and so much lack, why would I continue to have faith that my God would deliver me?

Through it all, I've learned to be defiantly hopeful. I've realized that no matter how big my problem is, it's not bigger than God. However, my problem IS bigger than me. So why would I cut off the only chance I have of beating this thing by cutting out the ONLY one who CAN beat it all because I'm frustrated or mad at Him? I can STILL be frustrated with God and dependent upon Him.

He understands our frustrations and our human shortfalls. For me, that is a sign that there is a true relationship with the Father. Name one true relationship you have ever been in that you haven't felt frustrated or angry in at one point or another. It does not make it right. It just makes it human. And while we equate being human with being flawed, we still do not get a pass to stay angry. You MUST be aware of your emotions always and refuse to allow yourself to stay there for too long.

My husband has always said, "Your emotions should be a gauge, not a guide." They are gauges that should show you where you are spiritually. They should be used as a beacon or an alarm if you are allowing your emotions to get out of sorts. Your emotions should never guide you. If you are allowing your emotions to dictate your life, you are making decisions on a" soulish" level rather than a spiritual one. And that is trouble waiting to happen.

For quite a few years I did just that. I let my emotions dictate my decision making. It wreaked havoc on my marriage, on our ministry, and in my own spiritual life. It's such an easy thing to do, especially when life has been so trying and problematic. You are so tired of being strong, and honestly, where has being strong gotten you anyway? But it's in that weariness that the enemy sneaks in. You barely even notice him because of all the other chaos and turmoil you're dealing with. But he's there. He's operating in your tired body, your weary soul, and your broken spirit. And I lived that way for far too long.

To be completely honest, I eventually just got really tired of being really tired, mentally, physically, and spiritually. I knew something had to change, and, since I knew it wasn't God, I knew it had to be me. So, I began doing some real soul searching. The direction for this soul searching had a strange beginning. It was an unexpected beginning because I was simply wasting time trying to escape reality by mechanically scrolling through Facebook, the most efficient time-waster known to man. I don't even remember what friend posted it or where I was when I read it, but it changed me and started me on my soul-searching journey. It is a quote by Pravinee Hurbungs. It read, "If you expect the world to be fair with you because you are fair, you're fooling yourself. That's like expecting the lion not to eat you because you did not eat him."

I don't know if that means anything to you and I'm not even sure if she meant it the way I took it, but it hit me like a ton of bricks. It made me realize that I didn't think the horrible events in my life should be happening to me because I was a good person. I wasn't just a good person, but I was a good, Christian person. Therefore, I didn't deserve for bad things to happen to me. Bad things should happen to bad people. And when bad things happened to good people, well, that's because they probably had secret sin in their life somewhere. (Yeah, we've all heard that awful phrase uttered at church more than once in our lives). But not me! There was no secret sin. This should not be happening to me.

After writing that last paragraph, I can see why God took me through some of the crap that I went through. Oh, the ego young "me" had!! I had to be stripped of that. Wow! Just wow!

But the realization that came next changed me to my core. I was using my 'faith' as some sort of bribery. Basically, I would have faith and then God would do His thing and deliver me and sustain me and provide for me. That's how faith works, right?

But the second that He didn't deliver on those things, I was mad and blaming God. I often thought, "I held up my end with the faith thing; now you hold up your end with the provision thing. It's not hard, God. It's a give and take. I sow goodness; therefore, I should reap goodness." While that is a true statement and a scripturally accurate statement, it has been misconstrued so grossly that when bad things happen to us we think God has abandoned us or at the very least, not held up His end of the bargain.

We are basically accusing God of being unfaithful to us. It sounds crazy when I put it like that, doesn't it? Yet we do it all the time. In our moment of weakness and faithlessness, instead of taking responsibility for our weakness and faithlessness, we begin to literally accuse our heavenly Father of being unfaithful to us. And that my friends, is a sure-fire way to know that you are allowing your emotions to drive you.

I realized that my faith was solely in what He could do for me and not simply in who He is. I was using my faith as if it was some sort of gift delivered to God and now, out of thankfulness, He must reciprocate the gift. That had to change. I wanted my faith to be pure. I wanted my faith to be so pure that even if He never did another thing for me, sending His son was enough. I wanted my faith to be from a place of knowing my Father's heart: knowing that He truly does have plans for me, knowing that He wants the best for me. And I wanted my faith to stem from a place of knowing that my Father's idea of what's best for me won't always match my ideas and that's okay. I will still choose to trust Him. I simply wanted my faith to be about Him and not about me and not what I expect Him to do for me.

Yes, I still expect Him to deliver me and protect me and provide for me. There is nothing wrong with that. But if you find yourself getting angry with God, believing that He has abandoned you, or that He is ignoring you when things in your life start to crumble, then you may need to start looking inward. If your faith is based more on you than it is about Him, something must change. If your faith crumbles every time your situation does, something must change. If your faith is purely about what He can do for you instead of what He already has done for you, something must change.

You have to ask yourself, do I really believe that God is good all the time or only when I'm good? Do you believe that God is good when your prayers aren't being answered? Do you believe that God is good when you can't pay your bills? Do you believe that God is good when you are crying out to God, but your marriage is still falling apart? Do you believe that God is good when you are battling depression, feeling alone, feeling abandoned? Do you believe that God is good when you are believing for healing, but healing doesn't come?

Do you believe that God is good during those times?

If you truly believe that God is capable of abandoning you, turning His back on you, ignoring you as you cry out to Him, or any other traits that He is incapable of doing, then you have to deal with some personal heart issues before you can move forward. Otherwise, that will affect every part of your spiritual walk, and you will NEVER be able to stand effectively against the enemy if you think that God is abandoning, you or leaving you to stand alone. This means that you are not dealing with the issues with the one who lives in you and through you, because you don't believe that He is there. That means you are doing it through your own free will. Tell me how well that's been working out for you.

My revelation that I was using faith as a bribe changed me. The picture of what true faith looks like changed me. And yet, I still have days where that revelation is just not enough. That revelation is glazed over by my own hurts and frustrations because that's what being a human being living in a fallen world with human insufficiencies and flaws look like. And so, I must pull myself up out of my own pity, choose to be defiantly hopeful, and start to stand once again.

And because He is far more faithful to us than we can ever be to Him, God meets us right where we left off, in the muck and the mess, and the tiredness and the pity and says, "I'll stand with you. And one day my sweet child, you will understand when you finally get to see the big picture."

CHAPTER 6

HELLO, DARKNESS MY OLD FRIEND. GET OUT!

Consequently, everything kind of hit me today. I don't know what was different about today than yesterday, but it was different in the harshest way possible. As thankful as I am that my son offered the money to us and as thankful as I am to still have running water, it is still hard. I am not defiantly hopeful. I am afraid. I am hurt. I am lost. I am angry. I am broken.

You may remember from the previous chapter that I mentioned that Fridays were the hardest for me because I know there is a 0% chance of a deposit being made over the weekend. But today is just a Tuesday-- a normal run-of-the-mill Tuesday--except it's not. There is nothing normal about this day. Today is a hard

Tuesday. It's been a bumpy, rough Tuesday. It feels more like a Friday, except maybe even worse.

My husband got up before me this morning, so I didn't even have to check my bank account to see if a deposit was made. The fact that he wasn't grinning ear-to-ear or jumping up-and-down screaming was confirmation enough that it wasn't deposited. For some reason, it knocked the wind completely out of my sails. It paralyzed me. I haven't done anything today. I COULDN' T do anything today. I'm way behind schedule. It took all of my energy just to hold back the tears, though if I am being honest, a few managed to escape.

I have lain on the couch all day fighting with my fear that another week might pass without any money. Some moments I was winning. Some moments my fear was winning. Honestly, for most of the day, fear has had the upper hand. To make matters worse, I had to borrow money from my son today to keep our water from being turned off. From our son!! That's not right. We are the parents; we are supposed to be offering help to him not taking it from him, not to mention how many times my daughter has brought food out or left money hidden until after she was gone so we would be forced to take it. I had to borrow money from my mom, who is on a very limited budget, to get groceries. My in-laws have had to pay for our car note the past two months.

We are grown! We should not have to do this! Plus, we worked so hard for this money. It's not like we are asking for something to be handed to us. We are asking for what is rightfully ours! We stepped out in faith to get this job and this money! Why can't we have the money we worked so hard for?!?

To make matters worse, the company that owes us, pretty much blows us off anytime we call and ask about the money. They act like we are aggravating them. They act like we are simply overreacting and that we have no right or reason to be calling them. I've tried to explain how dire our situation is, but they don't care and don't want to hear it. If we email to ask, it's a 50/50 chance on getting a reply, but even when they do reply, it is a blow-off response. We have spoken to a couple of different attorneys. They both think we have a great case. But one wants an astronomical amount upfront, and one wants to take 40% of our $25,000 when he gets it for us. Neither of those options are feasible. And so, we wait, feeling like a ship that is dead in the water. It is such a helpless feeling.

After struggling by myself for several hours and still coming up on the short end of the struggle, I reached out to my husband. I told him exactly how I was feeling. I didn't mince words. I didn't try to hide my weakness. I used the big words... hopeless, broken, despondent and angry, SO VERY ANGRY. Maybe I wouldn't have been quite so angry if it was just the job and money issue. But it was the job and the money issues on top of the church situation. It was the feeling that no matter how hard we worked or how much faith we had, we still just ended up at the bottom of life's trashcan, discarded, unwanted and unappreciated. It was the culmination of the last two years of heartache, rejection and disappointment that was trying to engulf and overwhelm me to suffocate the life out of me today.

I begged him to say anything that might make me feel better. He did. He knows me. He knows that most days, my faith is solid and stable. So, when I throw up my flair for help, he is quick to respond. He encouraged me, prayed with me, and just sat and held me for a while. But then he looked at me and said, "You need to go write this in your book. People need to see this. People need to see that everyone struggles sometimes and that's okay."

And in that moment, I was so thankful that God called me to live a life of transparency. I don't have to cry all day and then try to write encouraging words about how easy and simple the Christian life is. I'm called to be open and honest about living a Christian life in a hard, disappointing world. I'm called to tell you that it's not all sunshine and glitter. I'm called to tell you that some days, fear wins. It just does. I'm called to tell you it's okay that you have momentary weaknesses. And I'm called to tell you that EVERYONE has them. I'm called to tell you that even the strongest among us will sometimes feel weak, and that's okay.

I deem it an honor to sit here and say, my life is in absolute shambles right now, but my God is still on the throne--that today was hard but because I know who my Father is, tomorrow I will be stronger. Today I was down, but I will still declare that my God is good whether I have more than enough money, just enough money, or not enough money...even if I have to declare it through my tears curled up on the couch struggling with fear, because God's goodness is not dictated by my circumstances.

The key in life and in your spiritual walk is to get back up. Don't you dare let the enemy keep you bound in fear.

You are far better than that. You have been through far too much to stop now. And let's just get this clear right now; YOU may NOT be capable of making it through this, Oh, but the ONE that is in you IS.

I John 4:4 - You, dear children, are from God and have overcome them, because the one who is in you is greater than the one who is in the world.

So, you go ahead and lie on the couch. You stay in bed all day. You cry. You deal with fear. You deal with uncertainty. And you allow yourself to process. Then you do whatever it takes to get up off that couch. Tell your spouse to speak encouraging words over you. Put on your favorite worship music. Shout out His praise. Reach out to a friend for help. Or somedays, just let your tears speak for you. Whatever it looks like, you cry out to the Father. You stir up your spirit. You silence your fears. You remind yourself who and whose you are. You pick up your cross once again. And if need be, repeat the process tomorrow. And the day after. And the day after. And the day after. You have to be willing to repeat it until your strength and your faith returns.

Why do I share about my 'down days' or our financial lack or any of our other struggles? To some, my actions may seem counterintuitive or contradictory to a book about faith. Some think that when you talk about faith that it should always be exciting, encouraging, and uplifting. And oddly enough, in my own way, THAT'S exactly how I mean for this book to come across. I just refuse to surround it with fluff and glitter. I don't want this book to focus on my struggles, but I do want to show you that everyone struggles. I don't want to focus on my days of weakness but encourage you by letting you know that everyone has days of weakness. I want you to know that you will fail, you will stumble, and you will have days where your fear wins and that it's okay.

Sometimes, when it comes to faith, we focus most on the payoff, meaning the reward that you get after standing in faith: the job promotion, the financial shift, the marriage that's miraculously saved, the healing that was received, or whatever you were believing for. And while there is absolutely nothing wrong with that, it is also not the whole picture of faith.

Many times, we don't learn or acknowledge that the standing part is hard, that the getting to the reward is hard. We all need to know that the standing part can be grueling. People need to know what it really looks like and what it really feels like.

They need to be prepared for the hard journey, so they don't think they have done something wrong or somehow failed at faith when life starts to crumble. Because of how they have been taught or how they have believed, some people seem to think faith should be easy. It's not. It's just not.

But this mindset causes people to give up. They think they can never attain that 'level of Christianity.' No one should ever feel like he or she has failed at faith or that it's even possible to fail at faith.

My heart is that you know that you may fail momentarily by slipping into your human nature but that does not dictate your tomorrow. A momentary failure is not a lifelong epidemic. But even if you momentarily fail, at least you were trying! That means you haven't given up. So, keep moving! And if you fail again, just make sure you are failing forward. Keep going and keep getting back up!

CHAPTER 7

SHOW ME YOUR WOUNDS AND I'LL SHOW YOU MINE

When it comes to teachings about faith, we are more often than not, taught to just simply stand. Just have faith. But after twenty years in the ministry and a lifetime in the church, I have learned very little about what that actually looks like or feels like. Traditionally, we hear people say to simply press in and pray during hard times. However, I don't remember learning about what to do when we are so depleted by our life's circumstances that we can barely function to press in or pray.

People just rarely discuss these things. We don't talk about them in church. We hide those things away in secret. We put on a brave face and say all the right 'Christianese' lingo all the while feeling like we are dying inside. We have learned how to do this. Because unfortunately, transparency is not the norm in our Christian lives.

As a matter of fact, many times over the years in ministry, I have been advised by many well-intentioned people that maybe I shouldn't share 'quite so much" or be 'quite so honest' when teaching from the pulpit. I've been told that people don't need to know that I struggle. I've been told not to mention that my husband and I sometimes fight. Why? Do people think that we don't? Is there any marriage on the planet where there is not an argument occasionally? If so, I want to get marriage counseling from them!! I've been told that I shouldn't tell the congregation that I had a true mental breakdown from being so overly drained and tired (even though the message was about how God met me even at my very lowest). The point is, as a minister, I am not supposed to get to a low point. Good Christians don't do that.

I've even been told that I should never talk about the financial struggles that we go through because ministers are always supposed to be financially blessed.

I've always asked these well-meaning souls why they thought these things should not be shared from the pulpit. The response was always the same. It may be worded differently or packaged differently depending on who you ask but the general belief was always the same. "Pastors are to set an example for others. What will people think if they know our pastor is struggling? Pastors are supposed to give us hope. Pastors are supposed to pretty much have everything figured out. That's what makes people want to follow you." It breaks my heart every time.

I don't want to pretend that everything is easy or okay. I WANT you to know that a true Christian walk can be terrifying and hard. I don't want you to think that there is ever a level of Christianity in which you have "arrived." I don't want to give you something to aim for that is unattainable. That level does not exist. I never want to set anyone up for failure.

I don't want to be put on some fake pedestal pretending that I have everything figured out. I want you to know that I struggle. Why? Because I want to create a safe place where you can share your struggles with me. I don't believe anyone should struggle alone. I want to be in the mud and the muck with you. I WANT people to tell me about their trials, their fears, their shortcomings. I want to know exactly where you are, so I know exactly how to help and how to pray. I want to be on the front lines walking right beside you. I want to get messy with the people because life is messy, and ministry is messy. We keep trying to clean it up and make it look all nice and shiny, but it is a false exterior. It is a façade.

Now watch; I'm about to get super real right now. The name of this book is no accident (obviously). WTF, which in this case stands for "Where's the Faith?" typically has another worldly meaning that we are all aware of. Why did I name my book something that is so closely connected to such a derogatory worldly meaning? Because THAT is exactly what walking in faith can sometimes feel like.

Since I have been in the ministry for quite a few years, I have worked with a whole lot of pastors, leaders and teachers. These people are well respected and well loved by their churches and their communities. These people have a heart of gold and would do anything for anybody. They truly have a heart for Christ and His people. But I can tell you that my husband and I have met with many of these ministers behind closed doors and I have heard the original, worldly, derogatory, UNSCENSORED meaning of WTF more times than I can count. I have heard them scream it in exasperation. I have heard them wail it right after asking "What more does God want from me?" I have heard them say it because they were angry at God. I have heard them cry it out because they felt that God had hurt them. I have heard them sob those words through tears as they were broken by their circumstances.

Why am I sharing that? To embarrass them? No way. I would NEVER mention names. I would never call anyone out. In a strange way, I am always pleased when that happens. It may seem weird but when that happens, it always means that we are dealing with real, raw, honest feelings. They have been stripped of everything. They don't care about reputation or appearance; they want change. God can do something with that! It takes getting honest with yourself and God to move to the next level.

I am sharing this so that you realize that no one is immune to the struggle. People who are called to the ministry do not have some secret formula for an easy Christian life. They struggle just as you do.

So, if that is the case, why are we pretending? Why do we continue with the charade? I refuse to pretend. I don't have enough time or energy to pretend to be perfect. I will always strive for excellence but never perfection or even the illusion of it.

Subsequently, I have never stopped sharing or being honest. But, we have been so conditioned to believe that people in ministry are above life's struggles and we have it all figured out. If you just do just what we tell you to, then your life can be perfect too! Gag!! That nonsense makes me sick! And it is wrong, wrong, WRONG!

I will go so far as to say that this type of Christian mindset plays right into the enemy's hands. Because it has flowed down into the individuals within the churches. Now it is not just the pastors that shouldn't struggle but the congregants can't either. Good Christians don't have marital problems, or financial issues, or addictions to deal with. We have created a culture where people are embarrassed to admit that they aren't perfect. Sadly, that culture has caused isolation. Nobody wants to share about their problems because we aren't allowed to have any, at least not without being judged. Nobody can share their struggles, fears or issues for fear of being ridiculed. Nobody can cry for help from their peers or their leaders for fear of being labeled as unusable. So, everyone suffers alone in silence all the while smiling and saying all the right things.

But tell me this, in any kind of war, isn't an individual a much easier target for the enemy versus a unified assembly. So then explain to me again, why we are allowing our people to be 'picked-off' one by one just to save face and make it seem like we are spiritual experts who are above reproach? We will answer for that someday.

I refuse to do that. If I have said it once, I have said it a thousand times…I am one big, hot mess. I am flawed. I am imperfect. I am real. I am raw. So, I will tell you that with all sincerity and honesty that living a life of faith is hard, so very hard. Does it ever get easier? No, it doesn't. Your faith will become stronger. You will fall less often. Your weak moments will be fewer and farther between. And it will take more to cause you to stumble each time you get back up. But, each new challenge, each next step and each new thing you are believing for will push you even further than before because once you've mastered one area the challenges become bigger.

After all, God is the Father of Comfort, not the Father of Comfort Zones.

That's probably not what you wanted to hear right? That the walk never really gets easier? You're probably thinking that I score real low on the pep talk spectrum. But I want you to know the truth. We need people that will speak the truth. We need people to speak the truth so that people can be prepared. We need people to speak the truth so that others know that they aren't alone. We need people to speak the truth and say it is hard. We need people who will be honest and who will get messy in the ministry and in life. Yes, it is hard. It is so very hard. But, man oh man, is it ever worth it in the end.

Look, you can't say you're faithful without having been tested. You can't say you are steadfast without your resolve being substantiated. You can't say you are a warrior when you haven't been to war. And you can't teach me or encourage me about faith without me seeing your wounds.

I want to see proof of you surviving the darkness, overcoming the obstacles, enduring the heartache and forgiving the betrayal. I want to see your scars. The church body NEEDS to see your scars!

Only when we see your scars will we believe that you have EARNED the right to unapologetically and unhypocritically declare Job 13:15.

Job 13:15 - Though he slay me, yet will I trust in him.

Even Jesus showed His scars. When Jesus was crucified, the disciples' faith failed them. They questioned everything. They doubted what they had seen, what they had been taught and even what they had experienced. They were fearful and faithless.

When Jesus showed Himself to the disciples after the crucifixion, He said, "Peace be unto you." But they were not moved by His words. Their faith was not restored by His message. It was not until Jesus showed them His wounds sustained in the crucifixion that the disciples were euphoric and overjoyed.

Why? Because His wounds proved He was who He said He was. His wounds proved that everything He had ever taught was indeed true. His wounds proved that He had overcome death. His wounds proved that He had overcome hell. HIS WOUNDS PROVED THAT HE HAD OVERCOME! It was His wounds and not His words that proved it all!

We tend to look at our wounds as weaknesses. Let's get this straight right now; they may have been sustained in a time of weakness but the second you scrape yourself up off the ground and refuse to stay down, they become a sign of your strength, resolve and fortitude. They not only become a battle scar, but they become your battle cry.

Don't tell me about faith through theory. Don't tell me about faith through academics. Don't tell me about faith if you haven't shed some blood, sweat and tears in the fight. Don't tell me about faith while hiding your scars and pretending that the walk of faith is easy. Because your scars are what gives you credibility, your scars are what will let others know you are who you say you are. Your scars are what will give people hope that they, too, may overcome through Christ Jesus. Your scars prove that you are more than lip service. They prove that you walk-the-walk. And they prove that the Christ Jesus that lives in you is worth the battle—that the Christ Jesus that lives in you is worth fighting through the heartache, the devastation and the sorrow. Your scars coupled with your love for the Father will stir up faith in others.

So, if Jesus was vulnerable enough to show His wounds, why aren't we? If Jesus knew His wounds would stir up faith in others, why don't we? If we as the church are supposed to be emulating Christ, why aren't we?

Please, look at my scars and wounds. Look at all of them (and there are a ton). Look at the physical, sexual and emotional abuse that I suffered in my past. Look at the PTSD that I suffered because of the abuse. Look at the addictions that I dealt with. Look at the betrayals that broke my heart and almost took me out. Look at the affect that rejection had on me. Look at how I self-medicated trying to dull the pain.

Look at my suicide attempt. Look at all of my scars and wounds. But now look at the person I am today—the person God created me to be.

Don't look at my wounds to see how I was victimized but look at them to see how God took me from victim to victor. And watch me as I declare, *though he slay me, yet will I trust in him.*

Romans 5: 3-5 - Not only so, but we also glory in our sufferings, because we know that suffering produces perseverance; perseverance, character; and character, hope. And hope does not put us to shame, because God's love has been poured out into our hearts through the Holy Spirit, who has been given to us.

CHAPTER 8

HOW'S YOUR VISION?

I've written chapter after chapter about how hard living a life of faith can be. I've said how overwhelming it can be. I've penned repeatedly about how real the struggle is. So, why do it? Why not just throw in the towel? What makes it worth it?

Well, here is the truth of the matter. Life is hard. But life is hard with or without faith. Faith is what allows us to cling to hope; it is what allows to stand tall, to fight for what God has for us.

Faith is what lets us know that this is not where our stories end. Through faith we believe that there is better if we just press through. But without faith, it all feels hopeless. Everything is based on our own abilities.

There is no one else looking out for us. There is no divine intervention. It's just us. But our walk with Christ, which is an act of faith in and of itself, not only allows us to know that we are not alone, it makes our lives about so much more than just us—because in each of us lies a purpose and a vision.

God created each and every single one of you for a divine and amazing purpose. You were created for so much more than just floating through life day after day simply existing. You were not created to let the years slip by, wondering where time has gone. You were not created to simply punch the clock, retire and die. No. That may be the American way but that is not the Kingdom way.

He has called you to greatness! He has called you for a destiny purpose. He has called you for so much more than you even think is possible. And He did not call you just to get you to Heaven, He called you so that you can bring Heaven to Earth.

As you are walking with Christ, He begins to drop fragments of this purpose in your spirit. He begins to show you pieces of that purpose. He begins to show you vision. Vision on how that divine purpose will play out.

Now, our English language does us no favors. The word *vision* has lost some of its meaning and its weightiness. I am not talking about vision as a function of the eyes. Sight is a function of the eyes, but vision is a function of the heart. Sight is physical, but vision is spiritual. Vision is the ability to see farther than your eyes can see. The vision that I am talking about is the Hebrew word, *Chazon*. It refers to God's purpose and will being made known. It is an inspired direction from the Father.

Your personal vision is the most significant explanation of your calling. I'm talking about those hopes, those dreams, those visions that God has placed deep within you. It is the very reason that you were even placed here on this Earth. It shows the exclusive way in which God has chosen you to fit into His amazing plan. There is something so special about you that He thought that the Earth needed you in this exact time and in this exact moment. I know that sometimes we forget that, because life is hard, and faith is hard. We forget that we were created, designed and equipped for a specific intent and purpose because we can't always see past our circumstances right in front of our face. Nevertheless, we must be able to see past our circumstances to fight through our circumstances. Because He has something so spectacular planned out for you.

If you remember, in an earlier chapter, I mentioned that I had a very real, very severe mental and emotional breakdown. I was overworked and overstressed for far too long and it simply overtook me. This was not while I was some struggling, tormented young adult. This is while I was in the ministry. This is while I was pursuing God. This is while I was about doing the Father's business. There was just no balance in my life and I got stretched way too thin for far too long until I broke. I could feel my rubber band getting pulled tighter and thinner, but I was involved in far too much to just empty my plate. People were depending on me. And so even though I felt the rubber band tightening, I ignored the warning signs and pressed through. I kept thinking, "if I can just get through these next few months, things will lighten up and then I can breathe." But, I didn't make it through the next few months. One day, unexpectedly, my rubber band just snapped.

It was truly one of the darkest points in my life. I was in absolute despair and anguish. The strange thing is, there was no slow slide into the gloom. Once the rubber band snapped, I was plunged instantly into the blackness. It was like being thrust into a dark pit. The speed at which it overtook me was alarming. I did nothing but stay in bed and cry and cry. I shut myself off from the world. I considered any and every option to escape. I needed to escape. I contemplated suicide. I contemplated just up and leaving. I looked at one-way airplane tickets for one. A ticket for one, meaning even my husband, my best friend of twenty years was on the axed list. I needed to be away from EVERYONE. I needed to not have anyone pull from me. I had too many people pulling from me, but I had nothing left to give. Nothing. Every bit of me was exhausted and depleted.

My rubber band snapped on a Wednesday night. I was supposed to be standing in the pulpit teaching on Sunday morning. I had no plans of getting up there and teaching in less than four days. I had no plans of ever teaching again. I just didn't care anymore. So, for three days I lay there in the darkness. But as I lay there, hopeless and broken trying to find any way out, God started to remind me of the purpose that He had for me. While He hasn't shown me the whole picture, He has given me enough of the pieces of the vision that it is engrained in my spirit.

I would close my eyes and I would see reminders of it. I would go to sleep and be reminded in my dreams. God has so entrenched in me His vision and my purpose that even in the darkest place of depression, it was there. And a big part of my purpose here on Earth, is to stand before people and teach His word.

So, Sunday morning, less than four days after I was considering taking my own life, I stood before the church and preached a sermon about vision. I was, as always, very open and honest with them. I told them about the breakdown and I told them about the severity of the breakdown. Then I told them that the vision that God has given me for my life pulled me back from the brink of death. That in my darkest, lowest and weakest point, God still had a purpose for my life. Why? How did God's vision for my life pull me back? Because your vision shows you how God sees you. It shows you what He knows you are capable of. It shows you why you were even created. It reminds you that your purpose is bigger than just you. It shows you where you are going without focusing on where you are or where you've been. It shows you that you have a destiny. Your vision should empower you and terrify you all at the same time.

And THAT is what allowed me to break through the darkness. I was still torn and tattered and preached that sermon through brokenness and tears.

But I taught it from a place of victory — from a place of experiencing God's grace, and from a place of understanding just how important it is to grasp the vision and purpose that God has for your life. That vision and purpose will cause your faith to hang on even when all seems lost. That vision and purpose will be what causes you to pull yourself back up and fight through the dark places. That vision and purpose will make quitting seem unconceivable.

But the closer you get to God, the more developed your relationship becomes, the more of the vision He reveals to you, quitting isn't even an option. Your heart is so sold out for who He is, the purpose and the vision that He has for you, that the thought of ever giving up becomes unimaginable, even when quitting is all that your flesh wants to do. That vision strengthens your spirit while silencing your flesh.

And that my friends, is what makes the hard walk of faith all worth it. Your faith in God, in His purpose for you and in the vision that He has given you, will push you through the darkest and harshest of times. It will fight for you even when you have no fight left. It will direct you even when you can't decipher up from down. It will remind you that this is not where your story ends. It will remind you that you have a future and a purpose. God has so much more in store for you.

Proverbs 29:18 - Where there is no revelation, people cast off restraint; but blessed is the one who heeds wisdom's instruction.

CHAPTER 9

SUCK IT UP, BUTTERCUP! JUST DO IT AFRAID!

As I noted earlier, I don't have all the answers. I don't have everything figured out. There are no simple steps to follow that will ensure an easy life of faith. There are no steps 1, 2 and 3 that will show you how to live a battle-free life. No matter what you do, you will still have days that you struggle. There will still be days that you don't feel defiantly hopeful. There will still be days that fear triumphs. There will still be days that your human condition wins.

I can't give you a simple step-by-step instruction booklet to make that any easier. But what I can do is tell you that it will be okay. I can tell you that God never expects perfection from you.

I can tell you that it doesn't matter how many times you fall; it only matters how many times you get up. And while I can't tell you a simple step-by-step process to make it any easier, I can give you practices that will strengthen your spirit and help you stand through the hard days and the dark times.

These principles will help prepare you, strengthen you and drive you when times are tough. And even if you momentarily get knocked down, these methods won't allow you to stay down. They will push you to move forward even when you don't think it is possible. They will drive you even at your lowest. They will propel you even at your weakest.

I touched on one of these in the previous chapter. Vision. But I want to go deeper into the vision and purpose that God has given you because it plays such a vital and integral part of your Christian walk.

Vision is your ability to hear and perceive the voice of God. Vision is revelation from God at its core. Vision is seizing what is in the spiritual realm and doing whatever is necessary to make it a reality. Because when it is genuine revelation, a true vision of God is given to keep you focused, to define your purpose, to inspire you and to give you passion. Vision creates passion and passion motivates you.

I read a quote once by an unknown author that said, *"Vision must capture us before we can capture it."*

That means your vision must become so real that you are willing to commit your life to it. And here is where the faith comes in; you must be willing to commit your life to it before there is even any real evidence to show for that belief and commitment. Thankfully, our faith is stimulated and triggered by the vision we receive from God.

Here's the thing; faith causes action. Faith causes us to ACT on our vision. Vision creates passion, passion creates motivation, motivation stirs faith and faith causes action, and action because of faith, pleases the Father. If we never act on it and all we do is talk about it, then it is no longer a vision; it is a fantasy.

Hebrews 11:6: Without faith it is impossible to please God.

It is when our faith combines with our passion and we begin to act and function within our God-given vision that the Father's heart is pleased. And that is when you become dangerous to the enemy.

Why do you think he tries so hard to deter you before you get to this point?

Why do you think he fights so hard in trying to prevent you from acting on your vision?

Why? Because action taken, means ground taken for the Kingdom and ground lost for the enemy.

Action taken means saved souls. Action taken means lives affected. Action taken means the world feeling the Father's love in us and through us.

Action taken, means being the hands and feet of Jesus, and action taken, means we will no longer let fear, intimidation, financial hardships or any other excuse define us.

Action taken means God's vision has fully and wholly captured us.

So, if faith plays such a huge part in fulfilling the vision that God has for us, how do we stop just talking about it and actually start walking in it?

The first step is that we must know our TRUE identity in Christ. This is Christianity 101 yet many people don't truly understand who they are in Christ. Listen, there are no spiritual shortcuts. It is not possible to know what God has for you, what your destiny is, your God-given vision or anything else until you know who you are on a spiritual level. And I mean on a real relationship level, not on an academic level.

What do I mean by that? I mean, revelation of this nature can't come from an outside source. This is not something that is processed through your brain or taught by someone else. They can instill the knowledge of God's love for you but until that knowledge is absorbed on a very personal level in your spirit, that knowledge remains at a superficial status.

Look, if I ask you to tell me a little bit about yourself, you will start rambling off statistics; your name, age, number of children, married or single, etc. This information rolls off your tongue with ease.

Now, if I were to ask you to tell me who you are spiritually, does that answer come quite so easily? Does it come organically or is it recited?

Here is the test. Answer the question of who you are spiritually. Now ask yourself if you actually believe your own description. Answering this question will let you know if it is a recited description of yourself or a revelation description of yourself.

"I am more than a conqueror." Do you feel like more than a conqueror? Do you believe that you are more than a conqueror? Do you believe that through Christ Jesus you can conquer the very real battles that you are facing right now?

"I am worthy." This is a big one. Many people struggle with self-worth. Do you honestly feel worthy of His unconditional love—of His forgiveness—of His destiny purpose for your life?

"I am a child of the Most High King." Are you able to explain what it means to be a child of the Most High King? Do you know and understand your rights as a child of the king?

Answering these questions and others with the deepest level of honesty is imperative. Because if you don't believe these things, that's okay. It just shows you that you need to press into the Father even more and ask Him for the revelation of who you are in Him and the rights that affords you as His beloved child. No one can do this for you. You must do this on your own. But once you receive this revelation, your life will be forever changed. This spiritual epiphany alone will strengthen your faith in hard times.

The second thing to know about the vision that God has for your life, is what it looks like for you. You certainly don't have to know all of the specifics or even the big picture of it, but you should at least know bits and pieces.

However, some people don't know the vision, or the purpose that God has for them. Nonetheless, this information is crucial if we are to fulfill God's plans for us here on this Earth. We cannot fulfill what we don't know.

Still, for many, this is like a missing puzzle piece for them. They love God, they truly understand their identity through Christ, yet they still don't know what their purpose is.

And yet again, there are no shortcuts here because no one else can tell you what the vision is for your life.

You must seek His face for this revelation. This is information that can only be given to you by Him.

I will tell you that many people get frustrated and feel like they don't have purpose simply because they haven't discovered it yet. But I will tell you, that very purpose that you were placed on this Earth for was instilled and hardwired into BEFORE you were even born. That means your purpose and destiny was locked into your spirit before your mother ever even saw your face for the first time.

Jeremiah 1:5 – Before I formed you in the womb I knew you, before you were born I set you apart

You are not here by accident. You are here by design. You were literally special ordered by Heaven.

If you are still here on this Earth, it is because you continue to have a purpose that you have not accomplished. And your purpose is already locked inside of you. It is those deep passions and desires that are within you. For some of you, it's those hopes and dreams that you let die because of circumstances. But it has always been there, you just have to unlock it.

Years ago, God dropped something into my spirit. He told me to tell His people that to find their destiny purpose, they need to look behind their greatest fear or their greatest passion.

If you are one of the blessed ones, it is behind your greatest passion. It is something that God has instilled in you and the passion has just blossomed. But for many, it is behind their greatest fear. Why? Because if the enemy can make you too afraid to act on your vision, he can take your power away before you even start.

For me, mine was DEFINITELY behind my greatest fear. My greatest fear was public speaking. Terrified doesn't seem like a strong enough word to describe the emotions I felt when I had to speak in public. I absolutely hated it. I almost dropped out of Bible College before I even started because I found out that we had to preach in front of the class.

Long story short, through the encouragement of my husband, I stuck it out. And guess what, sure enough, I had to preach in front of my class. I was petrified. I anticipated the day with absolute horror. I considered calling in sick. I considered dropping out. You name it, I thought it. The fear was paralyzing. I don't remember the exact day or month, but I know it was a hot, hot Texas day.

But I still had to wear a turtleneck to hide the red splotches covering my neck, chest and arms because of my nerves. I don't think I heard anyone else that had to go before me. I couldn't hear them over my own heartbeat in my ears.

113

The anticipation of it was almost more than I could handle.

After what seemed like an eternity, my name was called, and I headed to the front of the class. I remember watching my hands tremble as I went to set my notes on the podium. And then I began to preach the words that God had given me. And guess what, it was powerful. There was a gift there—a true teaching gift that I never knew I had—a true teaching gift that I assumed I did NOT have because of my fear of public speaking. I will even go so far as to say it is a true teaching gift that I DID NOT WANT because of my fear of public speaking.

Not only was there a gift but there was such an empowerment that came over me. It was something that I couldn't explain at the time. Looking back, I realize what I was experiencing was the unlocking of what had been placed deep down inside of me. I started off absolutely petrified, but somewhere along the way, my fear became secondary to the word that I was preaching. Nothing was more important in that moment than sharing the word that God had given me to speak—not my fear—not my splotchy-nerve racked skin—not. my insecurities. Suddenly and unexpectedly, none of this was about me.

Guess what? I'm still afraid of public speaking. But at this point in my walk, I am far more scared of not pleasing the Father and of not fulfilling my purpose. I think I will always be afraid of speaking in public, it keeps me solely reliant upon Him. And it allows me to say this to you with no hypocrisy; if there is a gift there but you are afraid, then you do it afraid. If God has instructed you to do it but you are scared, then you simply do it scared. Step out. God will meet you there. He meets me every time I step up to preach. I am nervous EVERY SINGLE TIME until my foot hits that stage. Then because I am obedient even in my fear, He meets me there.

Fear is no excuse. And I am convinced that not only will we stand judgment for things that we have done that have not been repented for, but we will stand judgment for things we were supposed to do and didn't. I do not want to stand before Him one day and hear about all the plans He had for me that I did not even try to attempt out of fear, insecurities, worry or doubt. I don't want to stand before Him and say, but I was too afraid. Because His reply will always be, "But I would have met you there. You weren't alone."

If you aren't sure of your personal vision, pray for revelation and begin to look behind your greatest fear or your greatest passion. You have to know-that-you- know- that- you- know-that you- know what your vision is. Because the enemy will try to shake you, rattle you and break you. People will try to shake you, rattle you and break you. And yet this vision must be such a part of who you are that it can't be shaken, rattled or broken.

Nobody can tell you what your vision is. Nobody can tell you what your vision isn't. You can't figure out your vision from some self-help book. You can't figure out your vision from this book. You can't copy someone else's vision. You can't fabricate your vision. You can't let someone push you, convince you or persuade you into a false vision, and you can't let someone dissuade you from the vision that God has given you.

However, once you know what that vision looks like, you must protect that vision. Because that vision mixed with your faith is one of the most powerful elements on the planet.

Once God starts revealing bits of your purpose to you, surround it in prayer. And when you pray about it, be as specific as possible.

Yonggi Cho, the pastor of a million-member church in South Korea once said, "God does not answer vague prayers." I believe that scripture backs that up.

2 Chronicles 1:7 - That night God appeared to Solomon and said to him, "Ask for whatever you want me to give you."

Verse 10 is Solomon's reply - Give me wisdom and knowledge, that I may lead this people, for who is able to govern this great people of yours?"

Solomon was specific. He said, "Give me wisdom and give me knowledge." There was no vagueness. He did not hesitate. He did not need a minute to think. He knew what he needed in order to walk out the promises that God had already given him. He knew the answer immediately to the question. He had already thought it out. He had already prayed about it. This wasn't off the top of his head. This was taking time BEFOREHAND, looking at the vision that God had given him and figuring out what he needed in order to pull that spiritual vision into the earthly realm.

Solomon was direct and specific, and because his heart was right, God gave him the desires of his heart and so much more.

Another example to back up this train of thought on specificity is in Matthew.

Matthew 20: 29-34 - As Jesus and his disciples were leaving Jericho, a large crowd followed him. Two blind men were sitting by the roadside, and when they heard that Jesus was going by, they shouted, "Lord, Son of David, have mercy on us!"

The crowd rebuked them and told them to be quiet, but they shouted all the louder, "Lord, Son of David, have mercy on us!"

Jesus stopped and called them. "What do you want me to do for you?" he asked.

"Lord," they answered, "we want our sight."

Jesus had compassion on them and touched their eyes. Immediately they received their sight and followed him.

Jesus asked the two blind men, "What do you want me to do for you?" What?!? Really? They were very noticeably blind. Seems strange and unnecessary to ask them that, doesn't it? But He required them to articulate what it is that they wanted.

What would happen if Jesus were to stand before you right now and ask, "What do you want me to do for you?" Could you answer that question with precision and clarity? Could you answer without hesitation?

Have you already been contemplating how to bring your heavenly vision into an earthly reality?

Would you answer with only things that could meet your immediate needs, or do you have an understanding of the bigger picture?

Because if so, your answer will be a kingdom request rather than a 'self-request'.

Far too often, we don't really know what we want but we are frustrated with God for not giving us what we don't know that we want. We just want to Him to fix things for us. But we must be sure of what we want. Because being sure ignites our faith but being unsure ignites our doubt.

The next step is to prepare. God gives you the vision so that you can begin putting things in place in order to make it a reality. This vision is far too big to happen tomorrow. He gives us plenty of advance notice so that we may begin preparing everything, including ourselves.

What kind of things do you need to prepare? Your heart, your mind, your discipline…etc. Those things are a given. But how about the practical things? If God has ignited a passion in you to minister to the nations, do you even have a passport? If He has called you to a different career, have you researched the job market? If He is calling you to continue your education, have you checked into schools, programs and financing?

One of my favorite sayings is, "If I am praying to God to move a mountain, I better be prepared to wake up next to a shovel." This means that God will do the miracle part, but you better be prepared to work right along beside Him. We are to co-labor with Him. We WORK right beside Him. We do our part to make things happen. He may open the door and provide the opportunity for you to do missions work, but He isn't going to provide your passport for the trip. So, prepare for what's to come and prepare yourself for an amazing ride but not a free one.

God's vision will always push you beyond your own abilities and comfort zones. To say that it will stretch you is an understatement. But if the vision is not big enough to require God in order to accomplish it, then it's probably not coming from God in the first place.

God has called us to be visionaries. Your personal vision defines you because it aligns you with your destiny. It is the reason you were created.

He needs us to see what He sees. He needs us to believe that it can be achieved by co-piloting with Him. He needs us to realize our true identity as heirs to throne and children of the Most High. But most of all, He needs us to be willing, obedient, courageous and faithful.

It is our time. It is our time to step out in the revelation that God has given us individually and as the church body. We were created for such a time as this. So, let your faith arise. Let fear be silenced. He is our strength in our weaknesses. He is with us every step of the way. And if you're afraid, then do it afraid. He will always meet you there.

Isaiah 41:10 - So do not fear, for I am with you; do not be dismayed, for I am your God. I will strengthen you and help you; I will uphold you with my righteous right hand.

CHAPTER 10

COMPLAIN AND REMAIN OR PRAISE AND BE RAISED

Years ago, I started to really, REALLY analyze the Bible. I began to look for places where God promised us an easy, fluffy life if we just follow steps 1, 2 and 3. I couldn't find it. Believe me, I searched. See, if it was in there even once in some obscure passage, I was going to hold God to that promise! Unfortunately, it wasn't in there. In fact, I found just the opposite. So, I began to dig deeper into a few of the people of the Bible to get a better understanding.

You see, we read the Bible already knowing the outcome. We know that Jesus was raised from the dead. We know that David became king. We know that Daniel was saved from the lion's den. We know that Shadrach, Meshach and Abednego were delivered from the fire. We know that Joseph was released from prison and set into a place of authority. We know all of that. But do you think that they did?

Don't you think that these people of the Bible dealt with fear? Lack of faith? Their own insecurities? We often forget that we are reading about real people with real emotions. They were just as real and just as flawed and imperfect as we are. They experienced the same feelings and emotions that we deal with daily. Yet we read the Bible and tend to think that for some reason, they had it easier spiritually. Or we think they had some super spiritual strength that allowed them to do the things that they did. But the Bible paints a very clear picture of struggle, despair and hopelessness for many of the people that it speaks of. Yet we still think we can't achieve anything even remotely close to what the people of the Bible achieved.

We tend to be such a small picture people, but God is such a big picture God. God knew what the people in Biblical times needed to go through in order to be prepared for the next level that He had planned for them. He knew where they needed to be to fulfill His plans. And He knew the outcome necessary not just for the individual but for the nations because newsflash people, it isn't always just about us. Sometimes it is about the people we are supposed to affect. And just as God knew then about His people; He knows now.

So, I stand firm that when I have done everything that God has required me to do and hardships persist, that means that there is a bigger picture at play that I am unaware of. There is something that I am supposed to learn through this time. There is something that I am supposed to achieve during this time. There is someone I am supposed to align with during this time. Or perhaps I must go through this to be prepared for what He has next for me. Possibly, there is a piece of me that must be burned out during this process of suffering for me to reach God's big picture. Or maybe, just maybe, it is to gain endurance and strength in order to take my eyes off of the small picture and to simply learn to focus on the prize, the big picture, even if I can't see all of it yet.

Believe me, it is so hard not to focus on the small picture when you are living within the nightmarish confines of it. But here is what I have learned. Often, God will take you through some of the toughest times of your life in order to make you desperate enough to do whatever it takes to bring about change—to bring about those prophetic words spoken over you; He wants to bring about the big picture that He has waiting for you.

But how do we get there? How do we make it through those horrific, dark, small picture periods in order to advance to the big picture that God has for us? I have one very simple answer for you my friends. Praise and worship.

Praise and worship. It seems so simple, doesn't it? It's so elementary that it initially makes you want to discount that that can truly be the answer. It seems so simple, but sometimes we rarely talk about it. You always hear people talk about their prayer life but when is the last time someone asked you about your praise life? But our praise life is vitally important because our praise life affects our prayer life and it affects how effective our prayer life is.

Nonetheless during the midst of struggle, heartache and chaos, it is one of the last things that you feel like doing. But it is life giving. It strengthens our spirit. It straightens our spiritual backbone.

It puts fresh wind in our sails. It is literally the antidote for hope deferred. But read these next words carefully and get them in your heart. Praise and worship will not make your trials and tribulations any easier, but it will give you the strength to push through them, and it will give you the type of faith that gets heaven's attention.

It's funny to me that God is having me write about praise and worship. My husband, Ray, is one of the most talented and anointed worship leaders I have ever met. I am telling you this in all sincerity.

He has a true worshipper's heart. Everything that he does is done out of worship. Worshipping is not something he does; it's who he is. So, wouldn't he be a more logical choice for at least this portion of the book?

Not really. See, praise and worship is easy for him. He is gifted in that area. He is drawn to praise and worship. He is created for praise and worship.

But just because it doesn't come quite so easy for me, does that mean it is any less important or that I get pass in that area? No, absolutely not.

As born-again believers, this is something that we are called to do and should desire to do.

Now just to be clear, I'm not just talking about the kind of praise and worship that we get to be a part of on Sunday mornings at church, although that part is amazing and powerful. There is something mighty about corporate worship. There is nothing like it on the planet. I am not discounting this at all. But what I'm talking about is about praise and worship in our everyday life. And I'm talking about in your everyday life…being at work, driving in traffic, raising kids, cleaning the house, etc. I'm talking about a Psalms 34:1 type of praise:

"...I will bless the LORD at all times: his praise shall continually be in my mouth."

Here's the thing. We know how powerful praise is. The Bible is filled with examples of praise where we see His power released. There are grand stories in the Bible of huge things taking place because of praise and worship. Enemies defeated, walls coming down, lives changed, people set free, prisoners released, etc. But even though we know what a mighty, powerful tool that praise can be, it still remains one of the most underutilized weapons that we have.

The Bible says that God inhabits the praises of His people (Psalms 22:3). In other words, God "dwells" in the atmosphere of His praise. That means that if you are not feeling the presence of the Father, then praise. It literally draws Him near to you.

Here is what we all have to understand about praise and worship. WE get benefits from praising God! God does not have an inferiority complex. He is not a needy God that has to be told how awesome He is. He KNOWS how awesome He is. He isn't wanting you to praise Him to build His self-esteem.

Praise has a purpose. Praise is about recognizing Him as the Father. It puts an order to things. It gives us focus. When we praise, it becomes impossible to keep our eyes on the problem and it moves them to the problem solver.

When we praise, it puts God on the throne of our life. When we praise, we put Him into a place to move on our behalf. When we praise, we deny ourselves. When we praise, we take our eyes off of the one that is incapable (self) and put them on the ONLY one that IS capable. Praising is about us not being selfish. In a society where we are taught to get what's mine above all else…praising is about not being selfish. It is us putting Him first above all else…above ourselves, our problems, our insecurities. It is saying, "I will love you and praise for your goodness no matter what."

When we praise, our spirits are refreshed and renewed in His presence. We're strengthened by His peace and refueled by His joy. And because of that, we are far more effective when the enemy comes at us. Praise blesses the Father and in return He blesses us.

But here is the deal. We don't praise because we want something. We praise because of who He is and because He's worthy. Praise isn't praise if you're only doing it to change your situation; that's manipulation.

Praise is praise when you worship despite your situation. Praise isn't about you and it's not just about changing your situation. It is about inviting the Father INTO the situation. And when it's done with a right heart, YOU are what is changed. For through a heart of praise, we realize that God doesn't just change our situations and work through our problems, He changes us.

Living a life of praise allows you to have a new appreciation. You see through fresh eyes. You now have the joy of the Lord. Simply because you have become a Psalms 34:1 type of praiser.

"...I will bless the LORD at all times: his praise shall continually be in my mouth.

Something starts to happen to us as we begin to praise. Because we silence our physical brains - our fears, our worries, our doubts – because we stop making it about us and we make it about the Father, the physical side of us starts to shrink and the spirit within us begins to stand up. See, we must stop thinking of ourselves as a physical body with a spirit and realize we ARE a spirit simply housed in a physical shell.

Critical people become less negative when they start to try to live a life of praise. And honestly, you can tell where you are spiritually by how negative you are because praise and negativity cannot come out of your mouth at the same time. It is a beacon for me, a siren, an alarm that goes off when I start becoming negative or cynical. It screams at me that my praise-life is lacking.

So, as we begin to praise, our spirit begins to stand up. And as our spirit begins to stand up, our faith starts to build. And as our faith starts to build, we start to act on our faith. There is now an action that goes along with our faith. And when we start to move in faith we become dangerous. And as we become dangerous, things start to change and move on our behalf and to advance the kingdom.

Hebrews 11: 1-3

Now faith is confidence in what we hope for and assurance about what we do not see. 2 This is what the ancients were commended for.

3 By faith we understand that the universe was formed at God's command, so that what is seen was not made out of what was visible.

7-8

By faith Noah, when warned about things not yet seen, in holy fear built an ark to save his family.

By his faith he condemned the world and became heir of the righteousness that is in keeping with faith.

8 By faith Abraham, when called to go to a place he would later receive as his inheritance, obeyed and went, even though he did not know where he was going.

11-12

And by <u>faith</u> even Sarah, who was past childbearing age, was enabled to bear children because she[b] considered him faithful who had made the promise. 12 And so from this one man, and he as good as dead, came descendants as numerous as the stars in the sky and as countless as the sand on the seashore.

29-31

By <u>faith</u> the people passed through the Red Sea as on dry land; but when the Egyptians tried to do so, they were drowned.

30 By <u>faith</u> the walls of Jericho fell, after the army had marched around them for seven days.

31 By <u>faith</u> the prostitute Rahab, because she welcomed the spies, was not killed with those who were disobedient.

God in all of His infinite wisdom uses our praise of Him to change US and to change things for us! For us, our praise is all about Him. But for Him, that praise moves Him and unleashes His blessings on us.

Praise should be such a part of our vocabulary that it spills out constantly. Praise will lift our spirits out of the mundane, out of the trial, out of depression.

People always want biblical results, but few are willing to pay the Biblical price. So, I'm challenging you over the next 30 days – begin to pay that price. And it all starts with learning to praise in all situations. Some people say they don't know how to praise; well if you know how to complain, you know how to praise. It's the opposite of that. One is speaking death and one is speaking life. One is speaking negative and one is speaking positive. One is declaring that your problems are too big, and one is declaring your God is too big.

Begin to speak positive. Begin to declare His goodness. Begin to declare His will. Begin to declare things that aren't even seen yet. Begin to declare things from your spirit. Begin to declare over yourself, over you family, over your church and over your city. Begin to shout out His goodness.

And watch your life change. Watch your relationship with the Father change. I'm telling you, if people would grab a hold of what a mighty weapon praise is, we would be affecting society instead of society affecting the church.

And so, while I sit here still struggling financially, eating food that we had to borrow money to get, coughing, hacking and gross unable to go to the doctor, with termination notices threatening every single utility bill, a car we are unable to drive due to the lack of insurance, and cell phones that have no service, I choose to look for the big picture. I choose to praise God for the desperation that has welled up inside me. And I choose to praise God for delivering us even though it hasn't happened yet. Our ways are not His ways and our timing is not His timing. So, in the meantime, while I don't understand, I will praise, and I will stand.

Ephesians 6:13 - *Therefore put on the full armor of God, so that when the day of evil comes, you may be able to stand your ground, and after you have done everything, stand.*

CHAPTER 11

THERE WILL COME A DAY THAT MY BANK ACCOUNT IS NOT OVERDRAWN – TODAY IS NOT THAT DAY

Well, two days ago, we heard from the company that owes us money. For the first time since this ordeal started, THEY reached out to us instead of the other way around. Hallelujah! They let us know that they had finally processed the payment and we should have it in our account by the end of the week. To say we were overjoyed is a gross understatement. We were ecstatic! We were euphoric! It's now been 71 days since we received a paycheck. That's ten weeks since we have had any financial compensation for our work. Two and a half months since we have had cash in our pockets or bank accounts. So, the thought of the drought coming to an end was music to our ears!

That was on Tuesday. Today is a Thursday. My husband and I started checking the bank account early this morning and have continued to check it repeatedly throughout the day.

We were never disappointed or frustrated today by the same -$143 balance staring back at us because we knew there was a chance we might not see the deposit until tomorrow, Friday. Still, just out of excitement, we continued to check. The thought of it sitting in our account would not allow us to stop checking every hour on the hour. We were diligent.

At about 2:00pm today, we tried to check our account balance once again, but received the following message: *Account restricted from online access. Please contact a bank representative.*

We assumed that maybe we had tried to access it one too many times throughout the day, gotten a little over-zealous with our logins and got locked out. It's funny how we try to rationalize things away. Anyway, since our cell phones are still disconnected, and we don't own a home phone, we were unable to call. So, my husband went to the bank to see what was going on. He explained that we are expecting a fairly large deposit and that we need to be able to access our account online to see when it is available to us.

While the teller was looking up our information, my husband was explaining the situation and why the account was overdrawn and how the company hadn't paid us the $25,000 that was owed to us…etc. She was very kind and very sympathetic. She continued to look up information regarding our account and even made some phones calls. And when she returned to my husband, she dropped the bomb shell. Our account was closed this afternoon due to inactivity and a negative balance.

My husband almost fell through the floor. He said it literally felt like a dream. He couldn't believe this was happening. This couldn't be real. Our account that has been sitting there all this time with no activity and a negative balance was closed on the very day that the deposit was sent. What are the odds of that?

We had fought so hard for this money to come in. We had done everything in the natural and the spiritual to get this money that is owed to us. We had stood, we had prayed, we had believed, we've had faith. We've called, we've emailed, we've contacted lawyers. And on the day that the electronic transfer was sent, our bank closed our account without warning. No letters. No emails.

He all but begged for them to reopen the account but was told that was an impossibility. The only thing he could do at that point was to find out what happens to the almost $25,000 deposit when there is not an account for it to go into. He was told that it would be rejected and returned to the sender.

My husband immediately went to our neighbors to use their phone to call the company and explain the situation. We gave them the new account info and deposit information at our new bank. They said they will keep an eye out for the returned funds and then resend it to the new account.

The bottom line is, the chances of receiving the money this week are slim. The truth is, we don't know how long this process will take.

Ironically, yesterday, I spent all day locked away in my office writing the past two chapters on vision/purpose and praising our way through the darkest of times. I find it to be no accident that the day after I write those segments the enemy came in to steal, kill and destroy.

What did he think would happen? Did he think I would fall? Did he think this would make me doubt? Did he think this would steal my praise, extinguish my faith or destroy my vision? Did he think I would become angry at God? Oh, my husband and I became plenty angry, but not at God. We are BEYOND angry at the enemy. And I can't think of a better way to show my anger and hatred towards the enemy than by praising louder, longer and more vigorous than before!!

I will shout it from the rooftops, I will write in my book and I will declare that forever and always, I will praise the Most High King. I want my praise written in black and white in this book so that anytime the following words are read, it is a decree that goes out regarding the goodness of my Father.

Father, I declare Your glory! I declare Your goodness! I declare that you are mighty and worthy of all praise. I thank you for breakthrough! I thank you for favor! I thank you for your provision! You are the Alpha and the Omega! You alone are victorious! You are my Refuge, Redeemer and Rescuer! You are my Hope. You are my Peace! You are the great I Am! You are the one who sanctifies! You alone are worthy of my praise! You are sufficient for me! And with my whole heart I praise you, God.

So, I ask again, what did the enemy think would happen to me today? Did he think I would fall? I didn't. I am standing taller, stronger and straighter than I was yesterday. Did he think this would make me doubt? It didn't. I am surer of my Father's goodness today than I have ever been. Did he think this would steal my praise, extinguish my faith or destroy my vision? It didn't. My praise is louder, my faith is stronger, and my vision is clearer. Did he think I would become angry at God? Well, then that plan backfired, didn't it? Because it has made me not want to focus on anything but my Father. Not my closed bank account. Not my bills. Not my lack. I don't want to focus on anything that the enemy has his hand in. I refuse to be distracted.

There will be days that are hard. There will be days that I am not defiantly hopeful. There will be days that fear wins. There will be days that I am weak. But today is not one of those days. Today, I AM defiantly hopeful. Today faith wins. Today, I am strong.

To be honest, I don't know why this is happening. I don't know why we are brought so close just to have it snatched from us time-and-time again. I can't imagine what the 'big picture' is that God has for us that the enemy feels so threatened by, but I know I want it. So, I will keep my eyes on the prize.

I will praise my way through, I will keep my faith strong, I will respond correctly, and I will fight for 'the big picture' that God has for me. Because praise mixed with faith and right responses is what will get all of us to the big picture that God has for us.

Philippians 3: 12-14 - Not that I have already obtained all this, or have already arrived at my goal, but I press on to take hold of that for which Christ Jesus took hold of me.

Brothers and sisters, I do not consider myself yet to have taken hold of it.

But one thing I do: Forgetting what is behind and straining toward what is ahead, I press on toward the goal to win the prize for which God has called me heavenward in Christ Jesus.
I Corinthians 9: 24-27 - Do you not know that in a race all the runners run, but only one gets the prize? Run in such a way as to get the prize. Everyone who competes in the games goes into strict training. They do it to get a crown that will not last, but we do it to get a crown that will last forever. Therefore, I do not run like someone running aimlessly; I do not fight like a boxer beating the air. No, I strike a blow to my

body and make it my slave so that after I have preached to others, I myself will not be disqualified for the prize.

Let's go for the prize! Let's persevere! Let's run with purpose. It won't be easy, but it will be oh, so worth it. And if along the way, you feel you are being beaten and tattered, just remember, you're not alone. You are in good company. Keep reading.

CHAPTER 12

AM I BEING PLANTED OR BURIED? THEY FEEL THE SAME

The struggles that you are going through today are not new. The days of weakness you experience are not unique to you. The times of you begging God for mercy are not as uncommon as you may be led to believe.

These conflicts have been going on since the dawn of time. People have withstood tests and people have failed tests. People have overcome, and people have been overcome. You are not failing at Christianity because of your hardships. You are not failing at faith because you temporarily succumb to your human frailty. I know we can beat ourselves up when these things happen. I know that we have been conditioned to believe we are doing something wrong if hardships persist. But the Bible is packed full of stories of heartache, despair, frustration and desperation. The Bible has example after example of people begging God to have mercy on them due to their hardships.

David was prophesied to and anointed to be king when he was about ten years old. That prophesy did not come to fruition for twenty years. Twenty years!!! He did not become king until he was thirty years old! And during those twenty years he experienced heartache, pain, betrayal, and devastation on a level that most could not have endured. David was driven out of his own homeland by the very king that he served loyally and wholeheartedly. He was forced to live in caves, to constantly be on the run and even concealed his identity by acting like a crazy man. This man hunt went on for four long years.

This man, who was chosen by God himself to be king, should have been sitting on the throne but instead, he was hiding in caves, running for his life and acting like an insane madman. David had proven himself over and over. He had already slayed a lion, a bear and a giant. He had proven himself a fearless warrior. He had proven himself faithful to God and the King. He had served in the palace dutifully and dependably. He had proven himself to be fiercely loyal. He walked in faith. He walked in obedience. He walked with integrity. And for what? To wind up as a fugitive? A homeless man? A man hiding in caves just to survive? How many of us would have felt like God abandoned us? How many of us would have questioned the prophesy? How many of us would have been mad at God? Frustrated at the situation? How many of us would have called it quits?

Well, if you have ever read Psalms, you have seen that David felt those exact same things. My favorite example of this is in Psalm 69.

Psalm 69: 1-4

Save me, O God,
for the waters have come up to my neck.

I sink in the miry depths,
where there is no foothold.
I have come into the deep waters;
the floods engulf me.
I am worn out calling for help;
my throat is parched.
My eyes fail,
looking for my God.
Those who hate me without reason
outnumber the hairs of my head;
many are my enemies without cause,
those who seek to destroy me.
I am forced to restore
what I did not steal.

This passage is so incredibly powerful to me. This, THIS, shows what walking by faith can really feel like at times. It is feeling as if you are sinking. It is feeling as if you have cried out to God until your voice fails. It is feeling as if you have done everything to the best of your physical and spiritual abilities and yet you are still drowning.

This Psalm is so captivating because it is so relatable. Doesn't this Psalm sound close to the prayers you have heard come out of your own mouth at one time or another? I know personally, I uttered something close to this just a few days ago. The words might have been different, but the sentiment was the same.

But what I love about David, is he got it. He truly got it. Yes, he was devastated. Yes, he was frustrated. Yes, he was exhausted. But he understood that none of that took away from the sovereignty or the virtue of God.

Because while he cries out in anguish in pain, he then cries out in praise to the Father.

Psalm 69: 30-36
I will praise God's name in song
and glorify him with thanksgiving.
This will please the Lord more than an ox,
more than a bull with its horns and hooves.
The poor will see and be glad—
you who seek God, may your hearts live!
The Lord hears the needy
and does not despise his captive people.

Let heaven and earth praise him,
the seas and all that move in them,
for God will save Zion
and rebuild the cities of Judah.
Then people will settle there and possess it;
the children of his servants will inherit it,
and those who love his name will dwell there.

David was broken. He was tattered. He was torn. And yet, he would pick himself up, dust himself off and worship despite his circumstances. That is powerful.

God loves the praises of His people but when you worship, truly worship, in the middle of your brokenness, you garner the attention of all of heaven. That kind of praise and worship moves the Father.

Psalm 34:18 - The Lord is close to the brokenhearted and saves those who are crushed in spirit.

Looking at David's life, he was very obviously brokenhearted. He was very obviously crushed in spirit. But it is apparent why he went through the things that he went through.

Reading it in hindsight, I find it easy to see why God's plans took twenty years to come into fruition. When David was placed in the palace as a servant, he was nowhere near ready to be a king.

But God placed him in the palace, where at a young age, David could see how a palace runs. He could see the responsibilities of a king. He could see what worked, what didn't work, what was done right and what was done wrong.

While many of us would have been angry at God for placing us in the palace as a servant instead of a king, God was using this as a time and place of preparation for young David.

How many times do we miss the lessons and preparations of God because we want the big picture right now? We must be sure that we are more interested in being prepared to be king and not just in the position of king. One is about humbleness and one is about pride. One is about 'look at God' and one is about 'look at me.' One is about mission and one is about position. One is about the big picture and one is about the small one. But rest assured, because your big picture is about so much more than just you, God will not put you into the position of king (or whatever position he has for you), until you are PREPARED to be king. And if by chance you finagle, manipulate or exploit the circumstances in order to elevate yourself to king before your time, you will fail. Because once again, time means nothing to God, but timing means everything. Having a humble heart, focusing on the mission that God has instead of just the position that He has for you and trusting the timing of the Lord is what keeps us from jumping the gun. THAT is what works to keep us within God's timing even when we are questioning God's timing.

All the years of turmoil that David endured were not for nothing. He learned to lead, to fight, to be strong, to show mercy, to protect, to persevere, to be humble, and to rely on the Lord through the darkest moments. He learned all the virtues necessary to be the king that God required him to be.

That was David's big picture. It's easy for us to see it because we are reading it in retrospection. But judging by the Psalms, David didn't always see it and neither do we. It is so hard to stand and believe for the promises of God when we are dealing with so much strife and hardship. It's so hard to believe in the big picture when the small picture is consuming you. But God is preparing you.

David would not have been the king that he was without the trials and adversity that he went through. And we will not fulfill our purpose without the growth that comes from our own trials and adversity. It is okay to hurt, to question and to cry out to the Father. But, ultimately, you pull yourself up, and you praise God while you are in your cave!

Joseph is another one that has a story of heartache, hardships and triumph. Joseph shared with his family two visions that God had given him that showed his family all bowing down to him. Out of insane jealously, he was thrown into a pit and sold into slavery by his own brothers at the age of 17. His own flesh and blood. Let that sink in for a second. Can you imagine the betrayal that he felt? The hurt had to be unimaginable. He was taken from the only home he had ever known, separated from his father, thrown into a pit and sold into a life of captivity by the ones who were supposed to love and protect him the most. How many of us can relate to that deep level of pain caused by familial rifts?

Potiphar, who was one of Pharaoh's officials, bought him and he served in his house for 11 years. He served so faithfully and so loyally that Potiphar allowed Joseph to oversee everything that he owned. For 11 years Joseph loved and served this house with excellence.

That is until he denied the sexual advances of Potiphar's wife. Out of rejection and anger, she accused him of attempted rape. All the favor that he had worked so hard for was taken instantly by a lie. 11 years' worth of work, gone. 11 years' worth of proving himself faithful, gone. 11 years' worth of diligence, gone. And all because of one lie. 11 years down the tubes in an instant...because of a lie. And once again, that lie, that betrayal came from someone he trusted. Again, how many of us can relate to that kind of betrayal in our own lives?

Joseph was thrown into prison for TWO years not because of any wrong doing, but because he did the RIGHT thing and did not sleep with Potiphar's wife. Stop for a second and really think about that. He was an innocent man sent to prison because he chose to do the right thing. Can you imagine the frustration? The hurt? The betrayal? Plus, can you imagine having been elevated out of slavery, serving righteously, just to end up back in the pit? I can so relate because that is EXACTLY how I feel right now—right back in the pit from which I had already crawled out of.

We know that ultimately, Joseph was set into a place of authority to where his vision played out and his brothers did indeed bow before him. But Joseph was 17 when he was given the vision and 39 when he saw his brothers for the first time. 22 years of waiting.

In those 22 years, Joseph was betrayed, sold into slavery, lied on, forgotten and sent to prison. All of this was done even though he was an innocent man. Everything that happened to him was beyond his control. To all outward appearances, it would seem as if Joseph was a victim of horrible circumstance.

His situation looked to be dreary and disheartening. But Joseph was not a victim. He could not have ended up in the position that he was any other way. We absolutely must change our mindset. Far too often, we think we are doing something wrong or that God has abandoned us when the times get so overwhelming. But maybe, just maybe, He is positioning you and preparing you for something so much greater.

Joseph chose to worship God whether he was in the pit or the palace and he was ultimately elevated to the position of Prime Minister of Egypt, the second in command over the entire kingdom. He saved an entire region from dying in a drought. God needed him in that position at that time to save a nation.

He had to go through absolute hell to be put into a position where he could be elevated to a place of authority. His big picture was about something so much bigger than just he. It always is. We forget that sometimes. But God will take us through the most unimaginable circumstances to prepare us for what comes next. Because our 'big picture' is about so much more than just us, He must make sure we are prepared and in the right place at the right time to influence the ones we are called to influence.

But in order to get there, you must make up your mind to praise whether you are in the pit or the palace. Because if God can't trust you with the responsibility of being in the pit, how can He ever entrust you with the responsibilities of being in the palace. So, look at the last time you felt like your life was in the trenches? Did you praise your way through? Because the pit is where true praise and worship is learned. It's easy to praise when you are in the palace, but it is life-changing to praise in the pit. Praising in the pit, despite your situation, is the only way you will ever get to fulfill your purpose here on Earth. If you only praise in the light, then you are a circumstantial praiser, meaning God is only good when you are. But praising in the darkness is where true faith is born.

I could go through so many more examples of Biblical people and their struggles, their faith and their journey but I don't need to. You simply just need to randomly open your Bible to see it for yourself.

The Bible is not just meant to be read as a history lesson of God during the ancient times. It is to be a manual; an instruction guide that is applied to your life today. You are to look at their lives and their stories and seek out how it applies to you.

I hope these stories encourage you. They should give your spirit a much-needed breath of life. They let us know that our situation is not unique. The Bible allows us to see that our human weaknesses do not disqualify us from the journey. It shows us that our circumstances do not dictate who we are or where we end up. It proves to us that everyone back to Biblical times struggled with faith and understanding God's timing. You are not a defunct Christian by doing so. But most of all, it should give you hope.

Because even though their circumstances appeared hopeless, God was up to something bigger than their circumstances.

I have learned through reading the Bible and my own experience, God loves a good comeback story. He cherishes a great underdog tale. And He loves when there is no other explanation except, 'but God'. I was a prisoner, BUT GOD freed me. I was surrounded by the enemy, BUT GOD delivered me.

But to become a great underdog story, we must react correctly and press through. No great underdog tale ever started with, "I just sat on the couch and waited for God to move." It always requires action on our part. It always requires a right heart on our end. And it always requires us to be obedient, faithful and willing to praise even when it doesn't seem to make sense to praise.

What I love about David and Joseph's stories is that they both started with part of the vision being given to them. David was anointed to be King by Samuel. He held onto that vision through the turmoil, the destruction and the heartache. Even though he was anguished and tired, he held onto that revelation. That revelation became a part of who he was and helped drive him through the darkest of times.

Joseph's journey started with the visions of his brothers bowing down to him. This vision was not about having power over his brothers, it was about God showing Joseph that he would one day be placed into a position of authority. He held onto that vision through the turmoil, the destruction and the heartache. Even though he was anguished and tired, he held onto that revelation. That revelation became a part of who he was and helped drive him through the darkest of times.

But in those dark times, they both praised. The Psalms prove that David praised his way through his darkest times of despair. We know that even in the prison, Joseph was ministering to the other prisoners. So not only was he praising his way through his dark times, but he was teaching others to praise their way through theirs.

These two stories give credence and credibility to my two chapters dedicated to finding your vision and praising your way through. Both of their stories started with vision. God knew what was in store for them. He knew the years of stretching, growing and learning were going to be brutal.

But, He knew that vision would give them hope that greater things were on the other side of their hardships. He knew that vision would so encapsulate their spirits that quitting would not be an option. That is why it is so important to hold on to the vision that God has given you for your life. And if He hasn't revealed that to you yet, you press in, hold on and cry out for the revelation of God. Fight for it like your destiny depends on it because it does.

And then discipline yourself to become a Psalms 34:1 type of praiser:

I will praise the Lord at all times; his praise is always on my lips.

These two stories prove that everything that happened to them was by God's design. David could not have been the king that he was without the struggles that he went through. Joseph would not have even been in the position to be prime minister without being sold into slavery, imprisoned and being in captivity. We must make sure that we are not cursing the journey that will lead us to our destiny. Because no matter what God has designed for you, we all have our own freewill. It is our right responses to our situations that allow us to reach the things that God has for us. And cursing God and/or your journey is not a right response. You could delay or even thwart what God has for you by your words, your heart and your actions.

Just think, without the hardships that David went through, he could have very likely ended up just being a shepherd his entire life. Had Joseph not been sold into slavery, he would have lived and died on his Father's land. Do not curse the journey. You have no idea where that journey is taking you.

Our mindset must change from being small-pictured to big-pictured. This means that we don't get to focus on what is in front of us, but we see farther than our natural eyes can see. That means that when we are in the pit, we hold the revelations close to heart and mind. That means that we tame our mouth. That means that instead of thinking God has forsaken us, we know that He plans for us and a big picture is at play.

That means we understand that God is using these times in the cave to prepare us for something great. That means that we trust the timing of the Lord and truly grasp the revelation that time means nothing to God, but timing means everything.

Jeremiah 29:11 - For I know the plans I have for you," declares the LORD, "plans to prosper you and not to harm you, plans to give you hope and a future.

If you truly want to reach the full destiny that God has for you, you must learn to praise whether you are in a pit, a cave, a prison or a palace. You must be able to praise Him in the darkness and in the light. Yes, you will have hard days. Yes, you will have days that you feel that you have been defeated. That's okay. But then you focus on the promises that God has given you. You remind yourself of the prophesies spoken over your life. You begin to speak His praises even through your tears. And then you remind yourself, and the enemy, that this is not where your story ends. God has far greater things for you on the other side of this cave. The cave is not for nothing.

Isaiah 48:10 - See, I have refined you, though not as silver; I have tested you in the furnace of affliction.

CHAPTER 13

IT WILL COST YOU. HOW BAD DO YOU WANT IT?

Faith is the cornerstone of Christianity. The word faith is mentioned 270 times in the Bible (NIV). That would lead me to believe that God thought it was a very important subject matter for us to understand. But as important as faith is, are we able to define it? Could you explain it well enough that a five-year-old could understand? If a non-believer were to ask you to explain it to them, could you describe it in a very simple, comprehensible way?

Many Christians have a fairly competent understanding of faith even though they can't give a clear definition of it.

But I believe that it is important enough that we should be able to define it not only for others, but for ourselves because sometimes, when times are tough, reminding ourselves of what faith really is, can give us the boost that we need to make it through.

But to really define it, I want to start by looking at what it's not. Faith is not some abstract theory. Faith is not a feeling. Faith is not an emotion. Faith is not irrational. And faith is not denying reality.

So, then what is it? If you google this very question, you will get a plethora of explanations. Some descriptions break it down into eight different bullet points, the Latin words it is derived from, and are comprised of long reports and commentary.

There is nothing wrong with that. I personally, always like to break things down into the simplest of terms.

If any child, adult, believer or non-believer were to ask me for the definition of faith my answer would always be the same. I would reply that faith is simply taking God at His word.

It is merely believing that He will do what He said He is going to do. It is knowing that if He said it, despite your situation, He will do it. It is believing that He will always come through whether you are in a cave, a pit, a prison, a palace, a cubicle, an office, a church, a house, a car, a street, or a hospital.

It is seeing past what your physical eyes can see, grabbing ahold of the vision that God has given you and fighting for it regardless of what your current circumstances are, for no other reason than you believe what God has shown you and spoken to you.

Why did Noah build the ark? Because he believed God when He said it was going to rain. He took God at His word.

Why did the Israelites march around Jericho for seven days? Because they believed God when He said the walls would fall. They took God at His word. Why did Abraham leave the security of his homeland and everything he had ever known? Because he believed God when He said He would give him more descendants than can be counted. He took God at His word.

Hebrews 11:32 -31: And what more shall I say? I do not have time to tell about Gideon, Barak, Samson and Jephthah, about David and Samuel and the prophets, who through faith conquered kingdoms, administered justice, and gained what was promised; who shut the mouths of lions, quenched the fury of the flames, and escaped the edge of the sword; whose weakness was turned to strength; and who became powerful in battle and routed foreign armies.

Why did every single one of those mentioned in the scripture above pull off the most unbelievable feats? Because they acted on the words that God gave them. Why? Because they took God at His word.

Can it really be that simple? Can this hard, complicated walk of faith really be delineated to such a simple, uncomplicated explanation by simply taking God at His word? Yes, that is faith in a nutshell. But the implementation of it, well, that doesn't come quite so easily.

But when we are in the midst of hard times, if we just remind ourselves of the visions and revelations that God has given us followed by the words, "I take God at His word", our spirits will start to be refreshed. Admittedly, you may have to say it repetitively until you start believing. Again, the definition of faith is easy, but the implementation is hard.

I have been very candid and open with you about how hard the last several months have been. They have been challenging from a physical, emotional, financial, and a spiritual standpoint. Every single aspect of our lives has been challenged or changed. Some of those challenges, we triumphed in. Some we failed in. Some we are still walking out.

What I have failed to mention is that during all of this heartache and struggle, God has required so much from us. We are getting ready to launch a ministry, a church and two different businesses. So, where the financial aspect of our lives alone can at times be overwhelming and more than enough to deal with, God has me writing a book, planting a church, starting a ministry and preparing and planning for the start of two businesses once the money comes in.

The funny thing is every single one of those things are a part of the vision that God has given to both me and my husband. We just never thought it would be required of us during such an incredibly stressful and troublesome time. But God's timing is not our timing. His ways are not our ways. And time means nothing to Him, but timing means everything. And I know that we are not alone. Many people I have spoken with feel stretched beyond all ability and reason.

So, how do we make it through seasons like this? How do we withstand the enemy when we are too tired to even stand physically? I am telling you right now, the first thing we MUST do, is change the culture of the church. We absolutely have to become a place where our fellow brothers and sisters in Christ can find help and refuge in their struggling times. We cannot keep up this holier-than-thou act any longer. If God does not require perfection, then why does the church? It is not Biblical or scriptural! It is a façade, a charade. It causes people to be isolated because they are forced to deal with hurts, wounds and sins alone. If that breaks my heart I can only imagine what it does to God's.

Church should be a place where you can scream out in desperation and instead of ridicule there is compassion, instead of judgment there is love, and instead of rejection there is acceptance. We need to be place that will walk beside people who are struggling. We need to be a place that is willing to get dirty in the muck and mire because life is messy. We should be offering encouragement instead of hinderance and accountability instead of judgement. We need to create an atmosphere where broken people can be mended. We are required to be the hands and feet of Jesus, so we should be a place that people feel the love and acceptance of the Father through us. We should be a place that will lift your hands for you if you become too weary to lift them by yourself just as Aaron and Hur did for Moses. We should be a place that if you are too tired to praise, someone will praise with you and for you until you get your voice back. We should be a place that if you are too tired to stand, we will stand with you and for you in the gap until you get your second wind. We should be a Colossians 3:12 people.

Colossians 3:12 - Therefore, as God's chosen people, holy and dearly loved, clothe yourselves with compassion, kindness, humility, gentleness and patience.

But until we become a people of transparency and humbleness it will not happen. Letting people know you have issues, struggles and problems will always humble you. But pretending that you are above such things is nothing more than pride.

Know what the scripture says about a humble man? Know what it says about a haughty one?

Luke 14:11 - For all those who exalt themselves will be humbled, and those who humble themselves will be exalted."

Proverbs 11:2 - When pride comes, then comes disgrace, but with humility comes wisdom.

James 4:6 - But he gives us more grace. That is why Scripture says: "God opposes the proud but shows favor to the humble."

Proverbs 16:18 - Pride goes before destruction, a haughty spirit before a fall.

There is scripture-after-scripture-after-scripture that warn of the consequences of pride and there is scripture-after-scripture-after-scripture that speak of the blessings that come with a humble heart. But none ministers me more than the following:

Philippians 2: 3-4 - Do nothing out of selfish ambition or vain conceit. Rather, in humility value others above yourselves, not looking to your own interests but each of you to the interests of the others.

When we refuse to allow others to see our imperfections and flaws, it is for no other reason than looking out for our own interests. But when we humble ourselves and allow people to see us as we truly are, flaws and all, it allows people to breathe. It encourages them that they are not alone. It lets them know that it's okay to be human. It encourages them to reach out to receive healing without shame or embarrassment. And for me, that's more than enough reason to share the ugliest sides of myself. Because we are all in this as one and we will always be stronger together. So please, have a look at all of my human fragility, my mistakes, my weaknesses, and my struggles. Please, see that I am imperfect. And if my imperfect struggles encourage just one person to continue fighting the good fight then it is all worthwhile because my life is not my own.

I have found encouragement many times in the imperfections of others. I know that sounds like a strange thing to say. I have never celebrated another human being's weaknesses but when I see someone I admire openly share about their struggles, it allows me to see that I am not alone and that I am not disqualified because of my weaknesses.

When I was a young adult, I would watch all the pastors on TV (male and female) and see how perfectly they were put together, dressed to the nines, every hair in place, and preaching from a pristine stage covered in gold-plated everything. I never felt like I could reach a point in my life that I could attain that level of perfection, so, I set aside my dreams of being in ministry.

Then along came Joyce Meyer. I remember hearing her say that she used to lead Bible studies in her home while wearing Daisy Duke shorts and smoking cigarettes. And as crazy as it sounds, that ignited a hope in me that I, too, could be used for the Kingdom. It allowed to me know that everyone had to start somewhere. It allowed me to see that perfection or even just having my life completely together, was not required. It simply took an obedient heart and a willingness to follow the Spirit's leading. God used her flaws to ignite my faith all because she chose to be transparent and share her meager beginnings.

If God was looking for perfection, not even one of us would be used, but He does not require perfection. He requires faith and obedience. He knows our human condition. He created us, He knows our ins and outs, our strengths and weaknesses and overall how we function. There is grace for that. And making mistakes is far better than faking perfection.

I have said it over and over again, it is okay to fail. It is okay to suffer from momentary bouts of weakness. It's okay to be spiritually, mentally and physically tired. You are human. But I have also said over and over again, that it is not okay to stay there. That means that we must be aware of our weaknesses when it comes to walking out our faith. Do you give up to easily? When you give up do you stay there too long? Do you constantly complain about your situation?

For me, I am an incredibly independent person. I am also a doer. Both of those are great assets to have…until they aren't. Because I am hardwired with those qualities I will often find myself trying to help God with His timing issues. I will find myself trying to step out and make things happen. Now there is a difference between doing nothing and waiting on the Lord. But sometimes that line can feel a little blurred. We are to co-labor with Him. However, there will be times that He requires us to wait and do nothing. And I will find myself perverting the meaning of co-laboring with Him in order to justify my stepping out of His timing. So, I'm pretty sure that's why I am in a situation where there is absolutely nothing I can do but wait. Oh, the humor of God!

But if we are to walk the life of faith, we must be aware of our own strengths and weaknesses because I promise you, the enemy already is. He will use your weaknesses against you in a heartbeat. I want to take away as much of his ammunition against me as possible, not load his gun.

We must also ensure that we are doing everything that God has required of us. Look, as much as I say it is okay to cry and be human and be weak sometimes, that comes from a place of sorrow and exhaustion from the fight. That comes from doing everything that God has required of you, still standing, still believing and yet still struggling. That momentary weakness is a cry of the heart. But, if you are not doing everything that God has required of you, then it is nothing more than whining. It is done out a victim's mentality and not fighter's fatigue.

Look, if God is calling you to pray more and you give Him 15 minutes a day, that's on you. If He is calling you to dive into His word and yet you refuse, that's on you. If He is calling you to give a financial offering but you reject His instruction, that's on you. If He is instructing you to fast but you eat at the very first hunger pang, that's on you. You don't get to cry victim when you are victimizing yourself.

The walk of faith is not for the faint of heart. So, when He is giving you direction, it's always for your benefit. It is always to help prepare you for what's coming next. And you must know that it will cost you. It will always cost you.

John 3:30 - He must become greater; I must become less.

How badly do you want to fulfill your purpose here on this Earth? How badly do you want the big picture? We all want to hear, well done, good and faithful servant. We all want to be the kind of spiritual warrior that the enemy fears. But the truth of the matter is, none of that will ever happen without being a person of great faith. You don't have to be a person of perfect faith, but you must be a person of resilient faith.

If we get knocked down, we get back up. We must remember and hold hard to the visions and the revelations in the hard times. They will remind us what we are fighting for. We must remember to praise in the dark times. It reminds us who we are fighting for. We must change the culture of the church because we are stronger together. We must build each other up, be willing to climb into the pit to rescue someone and get messy in life and in ministry. We need to have a support system and be a support system.

So often, I hear Christians saying that they would gladly die for their beliefs, and sadly, that is a reality in some parts of the world. However, even though that statement is noble and honorable, for most of us it's a non-issue. Our lives are not threatened for our Christian beliefs. Rather the greater and more accurate question is, "Will you live for Him? Will you recklessly and tirelessly live for Him?" And the only way that you can honestly say yes to that question is if you learn how to live by faith.

That means you have to make it through the good times and the bad, the feast and the famine, and the favor and the betrayal while declaring God's goodness through it all. You will have to shed some blood, sweat and tears to stay in the fight. You will have to survive the pit, hide in caves and find joy in the palace.

You may lose some battles, but you can't afford to lose the war. So, yes, be willing to die for your beliefs but be adamantly determined to live for Him, and that can often be a far greater sacrifice than dying.

I repeat, there are no shortcuts on your spiritual walk. It will take hard work and dedication. It will take you standing and fighting for it. IT WILL COST YOU. It will cost you time, money, comfort, friends…etc. And just as there are no shortcuts, there are also no valid excuses. Being afraid is invalid. If you're afraid, do it afraid. He will always meet you there. Being insecure is invalid. You don't have to be secure in yourself to be secure in the God you serve. Being hurt is invalid. God is the Father of all comfort. Being wounded by the church is invalid. When God has called and directed you, no man, whether inside or outside of the church, can trump that.

We will all stand judgment one day and not a single excuse will stand, and no shortcut will go unnoticed. So, dig your heels in, strengthen your spiritual backbone and build up your spirit man. Become the fierce warrior that the Creator specifically designed and called forth. Remember, you are literally special ordered by heaven for such a time as this.

God is about to do something amazing on this Earth and He needs us to do it. He works in us and through us. He is looking for a people of great faith. A people that will not be defined by how many times they fall but by how many times they get up. I want to be one of those people.

Again, I don't have it all figured out. I still struggle and I still have days that I am weak. But, I will choose to remember His words, praise His amazing name whether I'm in the pit or the palace, send up a flair to my wonderful support system when I need someone to lift my arms for me, trust in the timing of the Lord and have faith in just knowing that there is a method to the madness.

And while I am no expert on faith, God is. And that's all that matters.

Galatians 2:20 - I have been crucified with Christ and I no longer live, but Christ lives in me. The life I now live in the body, I live by faith in the Son of God, who loved me and gave himself for me.

CHAPTER 14

THE FOLLOW-UP

Because you have walked with me on this journey, I wanted to fill you on the outcome. I finished writing this book last night around 12:30 am. Literally, within one hour of me hitting the last stroke of the keyboard we were paid. At 1:30 am, our money that was owed to us, was put into our account. After two and a half months of waiting, pleading, begging, fighting and standing, we finally received our money.

I don't know about you, but I do not believe in coincidence. I stepped out in faith, obedience and love and wrote the book that God directed me to write and almost instantly received what the enemy had fought so hard to keep us from getting. I don't know where this book will go. I don't know if anyone other than my friends and family will read it, but I do know I was obedient and faithful to the Father. I know that this book was required of me to reach my big picture. And so, my heart is blessed. I have completed the book AND we received our financial breakthrough!

But if I thought I got time to breathe from walking this through from hardship to victory, then I've got another thing coming. We now move on to our next adventures in faith—the ministry, the church and the businesses. I know that these will come with their own sets of challenges and hurdles. But because I know that we are doing this under the directive of God, I know that He will always meet us there. We are in a season of running and so I choose to run with purpose, perseverance and of course, the ever-challenging faith.

Matthew 17:20 - He replied, "Because you have so little faith. Truly I tell you, if you have faith as small as a mustard seed, you can say to this mountain, 'Move from here to there,' and it will move. Nothing will be impossible for you."

That scripture says nothing will be impossible for you. And while it may feel 100% impossible for you, it is not impossible for the One who lives in you. So, stir up your spirit, gird up your loins, fight the good fight and let's move some mountains for the Kingdom!

ABOUT THE AUTHOR

Jodie Austin graduated with a Master of Biblical and Theological Studies in May 2006 from North Carolina College of Theology. Pastor Jodie's ability to teach the word with her prophetic bent and real and raw style of teaching will unlock and stir up those dreams and visions that lay deep in your heart.

Pastors Ray and Jodie Austin have been married for 20 years, in the ministry for over 19 years and have two adult children. They live in beautiful Colorado Springs, CO and have their own ministry called Epic Life Ministries.

The Austin's travel extensively teaching at churches, special events and conferences. Their desire is to equip the saints to handle more, become more and do more! After all, the Great Commission was not a suggestion; it was a COMMAND, one that they take very seriously. Besides, God is far too good to keep to themselves!

For more information on Jodie Austin, to hear her teachings or to book her for a speaking event, please visit Epic Life Ministries at www.epiclifeministries.net

Made in the USA
Coppell, TX
28 May 2020

26607718R00114